# 10 Nights Without Sleep
## Cape Breton's
## Celtic Colours International Festival

"If I said your name, I apologize,
If I left you out, I apologize . . . ."

Lyrics from "Go Off On Your Way"
© Ronnie MacEachern

**Dave Mahalik** was a driver at Celtic Colours International Festival before working as Information Officer for 14 years. He is a founding editor of *What's Goin On* magazine. A long-time musician and performer, he is currently a member of the Tom Fun Orchestra.

**Murdock Smith** is the principal photographer for Celtic Colours International Festival.

I'd like to dedicate this book to my father

**Dennis Mahalik**

who got to experience the world of Celtic Colours the way I did initially, as a volunteer driver, and got to see firsthand some of what I do for a living. I am forever grateful for his and my mother Pamela's support in letting me find my way.

# 10 Nights Without Sleep

## Cape Breton's
## Celtic Colours
### International Festival

Dave Mahalik

with photographs by
**Murdock Smith**

Breton Books

Cover photographs by Murdock Smith. Front: top, Daniel Lapp; bottom, Angus Grant and Luke Plumb of Shooglenifty. Back cover: Paddy Moloney of the Chieftains watching Ashley MacIsaac; Carlos Núñez; and left to right, Wendy MacIsaac, Mairi Rankin, Natalie MacMaster.

All photographs in the book are by Murdock Smith with the exception of Buddy MacDonald with John Allan Cameron, which is by Ananda Kelly.

No one gets his job done at Celtic Colours International Festival without the help of hundreds of others. This book is a tribute to all their hard work and reflects some of our shared experiences. My thanks to Joella Foulds and Max MacDonald, to the production and technical staffs, to community volunteers and on-site managers, and to the drivers. I also want to thank the staff at Breton Books—Bonnie Thompson, Sharon Hope Irwin and Ron Caplan—who helped make this *10 Nights Without Sleep* possible. And also thanks to Krista and Maddi for putting up with me while I finished the book.   —Dave Mahalik

Editor: Ronald Caplan
Production Assistance: Bonnie Thompson
Layout: Fader Communications

We acknowledge the support of the Canada Council for the Arts for our publishing program.  Canada Council for the Arts    Conseil des Arts du Canada

We also acknowledge support from Cultural Affairs, Nova Scotia Department of Communities, Culture & Heritage.    NOVA SCOTIA Communities, Culture and Heritage

We acknowledge the financial support of the Government of Canada through the Canada Book Fund for our publishing activities.    Canadä

**Library and Archives Canada Cataloguing in Publication**

Mahalik, Dave, 1969-, author
10 nights without sleep : Cape Breton's Celtic Colours International Festival / Dave Mahalik, author ; Murdock Smith, photographer.

ISBN 978-1-926908-90-8 (pbk.)

1. Mahalik, Dave, 1969-. 2. Celtic Colours International Festival. 3. Music festivals--Nova Scotia--Cape Breton Island. 4. Celtic music--Nova Scotia--Cape Breton Island. 5. Musicians--Nova Scotia--Cape Breton Island--Biography.
6. Cape Breton Island (N.S.)--Biography. I. Smith, Murdock, 1972-, photographer
II. Title. III. Title: Ten nights without sleep.

ML36.C45M35 2013        781.62'91607169        C2013-905539-8

Printed in Canada

# Contents

Celtic Colours Photographs by Murdock Smith
between pages 62 and 63

# 10 Nights Without Sleep

# Because you gotta start somewhere, it might as well be at the end of the night . . . .

"Do you know any Cape Breton tunes?" asks piano player Doug MacPhee as a rusty-coloured spiky-haired Scottish piper plays the last note of a tune.

"Yeah, one or two," replies Fred Morrison, "written by a man named Dan R."

"Well," pipes up John Allan Cameron, the reigning Godfather of Celtic Music, "that's my uncle."

"No way!"

They begin to talk excitedly amongst themselves. Morrison, MacPhee and Cameron are soon joined by others, looking to get in on the discussion of tunes and relations. John Allan's uncle Dan R., of course, is the legendary Cape Breton composer Dan R. MacDonald. Doug MacPhee, like his mother Margaret before him, is an influential Cape Breton piano player who learned piano accompaniment at his mother's knee, and grew up listening to the most revered of Cape Breton fiddlers in monumental sessions in Margaret's home. Fred Morrison, a well-known Hebridean piper, is one of those rare fellows from the "Auld Country" who play the old dance style of piping—the style that thrived on the North American side of the Atlantic after the Highland Clearances, but virtually disappeared in Scotland. There is plenty for them to talk about. And somewhere else in the room another tune begins. The keeners know that's Joe Peter MacLean from Boisdale. And that attracts another crowd of musicians, crushing one another through the doors.

This is 1997, the first year of the Celtic Colours International Festival, and the conversation is backstage at the late-night Festival Club, one of hundreds that took place that year, in those nine days—a sort of prototype for conversations that will spring up time and again in the years that follow. The Festival Club is just the place for such informal talk. The Club is one of the arenas that make Celtic Colours International Festival a worldwide draw for musicians and music fans. The club concept is not unique to Celtic Colours, though it isn't a common experience at festivals in North America. Celtic Colours' Festival Club is based on an idea from Celtic Connections in Glasgow, Scotland. The theory is this: give the musicians a place to gather and enjoy one another, night after night, in an atmosphere more like the kitchens and living rooms of homes that cherish music.

That first Celtic Colours International Festival was hosted at the Holiday Inn hotel in Sydney, Cape Breton Island, Nova Scotia, starting on the Canadian Thanksgiving weekend in October. During the days and nights of the festival, twenty-five shows and a dozen workshops, demonstrations and lectures were held in small communities around Cape Breton Island, mostly in community halls. The festival opened and closed with major shows in Sydney at Centre 200, a transformed hockey arena that holds about five thousand people. The smaller concerts were scattered across Cape Breton, day after day, in Big Pond, Whycocomagh, Ingonish, Inverness, Englishtown, Iona, Christmas Island, Chéticamp, Judique, Glace Bay, Port Hood, Port Hawkesbury, Baddeck, Mabou, Margaree, St. Ann's and Louisbourg.

Cape Breton Island is 175 kilometres long and 140 kilometres wide, with over 1000 kilometres of Atlantic coastline and, in the middle of it all, the gorgeous Bras d'Or Lakes, a salt-water system that stretches across the island, just about splitting it in two. To the north are the Cape Breton Highlands and to the south the land drops to sea level. Sydney is on the south side of the Lakes, with a harbour that opens to the Atlantic Ocean. The drive to Ingonish takes you north for about two hours, crossing the Bras d'Or Lakes at its eastern outlet at a place called—what else?—Bras d'Or. Before you reach Ingonish, you have crossed the Seal Island Bridge that spans the Great Bras d'Or, climbed Kelly's Mountain, sailed on the Englishtown ferry for a marvelous five minutes, and crested Cape Smokey—the first of the mountain ranges that make up the Highlands of the Cabot Trail.

If you follow the Cabot Trail over Cape North, you'll reach Chéticamp in an hour or two. Acadian Chéticamp is on the northwestern coast, a French-speaking community. South from Chéticamp brings you through the Margaree Valley, still on the Cabot Trail. If you make a right turn off the Cabot Trail coming through Margaree Forks, you'll end up on the West Coast of Cape Breton and, continuing south along that coast, you'll travel through Inverness, Mabou, Port Hood and Judique on Route 19, also known as the Ceilidh Trail. But if you stick to the Cabot Trail at Margaree Forks, you'll reach the Bras d'Or Lakes again at Baddeck.

Now you're on the Trans-Canada Highway. Turn left and you're on your way back to Sydney; turn right and your world is opened to Whycocomagh, Glendale and Port Hawkesbury to the west. Staying on the south side of the Bras d'Or and heading west brings you to Big Pond and eventually St. Peter's. And heading due south half an hour or so from Sydney gets you to Louisbourg.

In Cape Breton we read the map a bit differently. Heading up Cape Smokey—heading Down North—fiddlers like Mike MacDougall and Winston "Scotty" Fitzgerald come to mind. Drive through Chéticamp and you might be thinking of Arthur Muise or Marcel Doucet. Place after place around the island is sacred music ground for the people who live here. The map might call it the Ceilidh Trail, but we know it as the home of Natalie, Ashley, Buddy, and the Rankins. North Sydney, to music lovers, is home of the Gannon Road and the Irish sound of Johnny Wilmot, Joe Confiant and Henry Fortune, and memories of Tommy Basker. Say Washabuck, and we're thinking of the roots of the Barra MacNeils. Big Pond means Rita MacNeil.

And into all that we already love comes the Celtic Colours International Festival, inviting names we've never heard of, as well as the already famous—instantly recognizable regardless of your

Celtic music literacy—like The Chieftains, probably the best-known group of Irish traditional musicians, and Leahy, an Ontario group of attractive brothers and sisters who would fit in as easily on music video channels as on *Don Messer's Jubilee*.

Hardcore Celtic music fans were more likely than the general population to recognize the names and appreciate the music of folks like Irish accordionist Sharon Shannon, the Scottish group Capercaillie, the four amazing Irish women in Bumblebees, and the Hebridean-style Scottish piper Fred Morrison.

That first festival also included many of Cape Breton's local heroes, like fiddlers Buddy MacMaster, Jerry Holland, Brenda Stubbert and Carl MacKenzie, singer and Celtic guitar pioneer John Allan Cameron, and pianists Doug MacPhee and Maybelle Chisholm MacQueen. It was a great mix of talent that spanned generations from the up-and-coming Northside band Slainte Mhath, whose sound relied as much on the pop music of the radio as on their ancestors' Scottish island home of Barra, to the indefatigable institution of The Chieftains, who were celebrating their thirty-fifth year.

Then there's me. In 1997, I was publisher and editor of two arts-and-entertainment publications—a magazine and a weekly guide—both called *What's Goin On*. We previewed the Celtic Colours International Festival, which was taking place at the same time as Cape Breton's pre-eminent underground/independent music festival Gobblefest, then going into its fourth year. Unlike the nine-day marathon of Celtic Colours, Gobblefest was a Thanksgiving weekend affair, originally conceived as a fundraiser for Cape Breton University's campus radio project CAPR, to buy a transmitter and get CAPR on the public airwaves.

I played onstage at Gobblefest in a band sometimes known as Boothead, and as a twenty-two-year-old bass guitar player, indie/underground/original music was more my scene than what was being presented by Celtic Colours. The magazines I published weren't exactly "anti-Celtic/Traditional," but they did present an alternative view—and part of the editorial mandate was to go beyond the obvious, to bring attention to lesser-known local writers, actors, dancers and the arts on Cape Breton Island. Music was still the island's best-known export. And rightly so. Our deeply-rooted traditional music was certainly spreading around the world, the sounds of Gaelic and fiddling reverberating in unlikely places, and giving Cape Breton a world-wide reputation as its unique source.

But this was only part of Cape Breton's music. There was a whole other world that appealed to people. Minglewood Band's country and blues struck a homesick chord with Maritimers across the country in the late 1970s and through the 1980s when yet another generation had to move away from home looking for work. Realworld's radio-friendly pop hits of the late 1980s and early '90s bridged the gap between what kids were listening to on the radio and the bands you could dance to locally. And Sunfish's mid-'90s, alternative interpretation of storytelling songs for the next generation provided something fresh for Cape Breton's MTV generation. In some places, mostly rural, the cassette sound of fiddles drowned out whatever the rest of the world was listening to, but in the industrial towns of the island, it was harder to hear the fiddle and the Gaelic with the TV tuned in to the Video Hits channel and turned up loud.

I know these divisions are just too simplistic. Some people listened with both ears. We have to remember Ashley, Natalie, and so many other young fiddlers were honing their chops, surrounded by both terrific old-time fiddlers and the world of rock-and-roll.

And the organizers of Celtic Colours certainly did not come out of nowhere. Max MacDonald had been lead singer of Buddy and the Boys, a winning blend of rock-and-roll, country, John Prine and The Band. Joella Foulds toured as an essential part of Rita MacNeil's band. And year after year, Cape Bretoners flocked to the annual performances of the Summertime Revue, where both Rita MacNeil and Natalie MacMaster learned to overcome their shyness. Still, when Max MacDonald and Joella Foulds made their plans for Celtic Colours, they knew the heart of it all would be rooted in Cape Breton's traditional music.

*What's Goin On* magazine was over two years old when Celtic Colours rolled around, and we were keen to establish our magazine as *the* source for local arts and entertainment news, reviews and information here in Cape Breton. In the September/October 1997 issue, Iain Kenneth MacLeod—a regular contributor and a future Information Officer of the Festival—wrote a "Celtic Colours User's Guide" which correctly pointed out that no matter how hard you try, there's just no way to see everything that Celtic Colours has to offer and, plan as you will, sometimes you may just be better off flipping a coin. We took that advice seriously. I offered Celtic Colours assignments to anyone who wanted them, knowing that just one or two people would not be able to capture the scope of this thing. Seven people contributed stories or reviews and we published photos from five photographers, putting the nine nights of Celtic Colours on the cover of *WGO Weekly* for three weeks in a row. That year, *What's Goin On*'s coverage of Celtic Colours was the most extensive and comprehensive of any media outlet. The two-year-old, independently-published-on-a-shoestring-budget magazine, run by a guy whose application to Journalism School was rejected, outdid the hundred-year-old daily newspaper and the local outlet of the publicly-funded national broadcaster—by a long shot. *What's Goin On* set the bar high right out of the gate for other publications covering the festival in subsequent years.

I got close to the action by volunteering to drive for Celtic Colours in 1997. I knew some of the players and organizers, and I wanted to get involved with something I felt was going to be a fairly big deal. Also, I like being on the inside. I was used to the atmosphere backstage, having been a child performer as a member of Barvinok, the Ukrainian folk dancing troupe in Cape Breton. I performed with them from five to about twenty years of age, and also played rock music and covered entertainment events with *What's Goin On*. As I said, this Celtic music wasn't exactly my scene, but it was all about music, performers and entertainment, and I'd learned early on through dancing that, contrary to popular belief, the folk scene was a lot cooler than most people thought. The family-oriented performances of Barvinok fronted a fair bit of rock-and-roll lifestyle and behaviour, but that's a story for another day. In short, I wanted to be able to hang out backstage during Celtic Colours, but I also wanted to be useful.

My time was limited with two publications on the go, so I stuck to a day-on/day-off schedule that first year. With the Holiday Inn in Sydney as Festival headquarters, I could easily drop in every other day for my assignments. My mission was to drive artists to their soundchecks and gigs, hang out, then drive them back to the hotel. Mostly, I drove the Bumblebees—four fabulous women from Ireland who played tunes like I could never have imagined. I have known lots of music, all kinds, and I've seen plenty of fine players, and I've never been afraid to be awestruck by what I heard and saw—but only a very few times have I been so captivated by music that I had never heard before that I couldn't wait for one set to be over in the hopes that the players would play something else as strange and new that I had never heard before, just knowing that it too would be as amazing. It's like discovering something that touches you deeply, shapes your face into that goofy grins that's obvious to everyone but yourself until your face starts to hurt, or draws tears until they're streaming down your face. The Bumblebees made music like that—music instantly familiar and recognizable, though you could not possibly have ever heard it before.

Wherever we went, I saw crowds quickly warm up to Bumblebees' exuberance for playing. With harp, banjo, mandolin, bass mandola, piano accordion and as many as three fiddles among the four of them, you know you're going somewhere musical when this quartet takes to the stage. As they played, melodies jumped out and the rhythm carried it along, sometimes surprising you with a turn or a phrase from their diverse repertoire that included Irish, Scottish, French-Canadian, Cape Breton, Cajun and original tunes. For the 'Bees, music is simply a part of life. It's obvious in watching them play. They fling it about among themselves, laughing when they fall off it somewhere along the way, and gathering it back up when they're ready. They live for the music and are always up for a session, no matter how late into the night the session may go.

I had met Bumblebees fiddler Liz Doherty years earlier when she was in Cape Breton researching her University of Limerick dissertation entitled *The Paradox of the Periphery—Evolution of The Cape Breton Fiddle Tradition 1929-1995*. We were friends already so it made sense that I would be their driver, and it wasn't long before friendships were formed with the rest of the Bumblebees—harpist Laoise Kelly, accordion player Colette O'Leary, and Mary Shannon who played fiddle, mandolin and tenor banjo. Laoise and I made quick friends—she rolled her own smokes and I had usually smoked all mine. She was always ready to "go for a fag." I guess my personality and my willingness to let the night go on until it was over matched theirs. We all would be there after just about everyone else had turned in for the night or wandered off. Hanging out with these four would set the standard for years. They were mad about the music in a way I'd never seen before. They'd play all night long and be game to go at it again the next day, and the next day, and the next day. This is what they did. They played music, and being in Cape Breton for Celtic Colours was like having their own playground.

I was finishing up some work at the *What's Goin On* office when the phone rang. "Dave, the Bumblebees want to go to Gordie Sampson's party in Big Pond after their show in Ingonish. Can you pick them up at the Holiday Inn in Sydney around midnight?"

Starting at midnight and heading to a party at my friends' house? Sounds like my kind of job. This is going to be fun. Even though I had eight hours or so until I was needed, I had been bitten by the bug and knew I would get no more work done that day, so I headed to the Holiday Inn just to see what was going on. The main lobby was alive with activity—people coming and going with armloads of instruments and luggage, luggage trolleys piled high with the familiar shapes of guitar and fiddle cases, people checking into the front desk with odd accents, and lots of stretching limbs after transatlantic flights and long drives from the Halifax International Airport, five hours away. Ready to get in on the action, I made my way downstairs. Tables were set up to distribute information to artists and volunteers. I said hello to my fellow troops, many of whom I knew from past musical experiences or who had volunteered during the East Coast Music Awards when they were held in Sydney in 1995. So I hung around for a while, soaking up the atmosphere, going out for a smoke to catch up with people, and making myself useful where I could before heading off home for a meal and a nap in anticipation of what I was sure would be a long night ahead.

That first mission to the house in Big Pond that Gordie Sampson shared with friends and fellow musicians Matt Foulds and Carlo Spinazzola—for the party after a show called "Winston's Classic Cuts" at the Big Pond Fire Hall—brought Celtic Colours to life for me. It may not have been my kind of music, but it was my kind of party.

The house was jammed to the rafters as music and dancing took over the clock. I couldn't imagine how Laoise Kelly's harp was going to perform at a kitchen party, but she parked it right next to the table and dug into the tunes with Gordie and Stuart Cameron on guitar, Liz on the fiddle, Colette O'Leary playing accordion and Matt Foulds on hand percussion. For the next couple of hours, you could barely move through the kitchen, but the music danced through the old farmhouse.

At one point I was upstairs in line for the bathroom, and it sounded like someone was pounding away on an old piano. I mentioned to the next person in line that it sounded like Sheumas MacNeil was really drivin' 'er now. When my line-mate asked when Sheumas had arrived, it occurred to me that there was no piano in this house. As I listened closely, I realized it was Laoise's harp I was hearing, chording along to the tunes like a Cape Breton piano. And never again would I worry about how an Irish musician would make out at a party in Cape Breton with any kind of instrument.

I had been to quite a few parties at this house, with most of the same people, but this one was different. Parties with this crowd of locals—Gordie, Carlo, Matt, Stuart—usually had a strong musical component. Playing music went pretty naturally with drinking and smoking, and we were all pretty good at it by now. On this night though, there was a sense of discovery. The usual cast of characters had been infiltrated by an unknown cast of characters, and there was no easy way of knowing hosts from guests. The humour, music, and willful consumption were shared by all equally. And it all centred around the music, which itself was elevated by the focus it held in the room, among those playing around the table and those standing at the edges. Although the players came from different countries and had as much in common musically as not, and the collection of instruments—guitar, harp, fiddle, accordion, hand-drums—was exotic by Cape Breton standards and not typical of the kind of session common to this kind of party, still there was a sense of shared tradition. Tunes led by Laoise and Liz and Colette were picked up by Gordie and Stuart and Carlo, who infused them with their own flavours—Carlo's all-feeling soul and down-and-out blues; Gordie's fresh absorption of traditional tunes plus his keen sense of popular culture; Stuart's musical heritage and recent emergence into the world of his father, John Allan Cameron. It all added up on that night in Big Pond.

Long after everyone else had turned in for the night—with the blinds drawn against the early morning sun—Laoise and Colette called for one more "choon," but the few who were still resisting sleep no longer possessed the faculties to take on such a task. And I don't think Laoise and Colette were much up to the task at this point either, just wanted to listen to someone else play. I did pick up Colette's accordion, thinking that the years of piano lessons my folks had insisted on—which I never really took very seriously— might allow me to pick out a tune or two, but it wasn't long before I gave up and acknowledged that my parents were right, that someday I would appreciate their pressure. Finally Colette and

Laoise went to bed and I went to sleep on the floor. And for me, the festival was really and truly under way.

For Joella Foulds and Max MacDonald, directors and founders of Celtic Colours International Festival, my Saturday night in Big Pond was two years in the making. They had established Rave Entertainment in 1995, and took on the task of artist and event management. After a successful attempt to bring the East Coast Music Awards to Sydney in 1995, their thoughts turned to producing more large-scale music events in Cape Breton. They were interviewed by Tom Knapp in 2004.

Tom wrote: "Hitching onto Nova Scotia's 'A Year of Music' promotion that year, the two wracked their brains for the proper Cape Breton hook. After all, Max said, 'We had the Rankins, Natalie, Ashley—a lot of Cape Breton artists were touring the world. We thought we could do it in reverse: instead of sending our artists out, let's bring the audience in.' Once they had a core of musicians lending support, 'we knew we had to do it,' Max said. 'Nothing could stop us.'

"But a big music festival isn't made in a day. To research the proper way to do things, the team looked to one of the biggest and brightest stars in the Celtic music firmament: Celtic Connections, a venerable and highly successful yearly festival in Glasgow, Scotland. 'We raised some money and found our way to Glasgow in January 1996 to meet people and hear musicians,' Max said. Then Max and Joella came home and started making plans—and contacts.

"'The festival that now exists is the same concept we came up with almost immediately,' Max recalled. 'We were trying to create an experience, something more than just going to a concert. It's about becoming part of a community.'"

Rather than centre only on big stadium productions, the Celtic Colours concept was to present the music in the communities where much of it traditionally existed and continues to thrive, closer to the home-and-local-concert context—the world that has allowed it to survive and develop over generations. Joella and Max wanted to deliver an experience that included workshops about the music and learning opportunities with master musicians—plus a Festival Club as well as concerts, featuring visiting musicians in league with local favourites. Through it all, Max and Joella carried a keen awareness that turning culture into a commodity can change the culture, can even destroy it. The festival would present new talent and pay homage to those who had gone before, keeping the old ways alive while inviting a daring mix of related cultures—praying it was all to the good.

"This festival must reflect the way we celebrate our culture. And it must take care not to change that in any way. What we have here is very special," said Joella in a 1997 press release. "We've asked Cape Breton performers to host all of the events and welcome the visitors into our cultural home."

And having the events scattered all around the island during the colourful autumn season would guarantee a unique experience for tourists, allowing them to experience the natural beauty of Cape Breton Island, so often used by the tourism industry as a selling point. And if it worked, it would boost the island's economy at a time of year when tourism operators would otherwise be closing up shop. The local artists would draw tourists; the international artists would draw locals.

**And so, after all the planning, organizing, negotiating, fundraising and publicizing, the Celtic Colours International Festival kicked off with a concert at Centre 200 in Sydney on October 10, 1997.**

Celebrating Irish-Cape Breton collaborations past and present, "*Fosgail an Fhéis!*—Open The Festival!"—deliberately showcased instrumental, vocal and dance styles featuring The Chieftains and Sharon Shannon from Ireland and Cape Breton's Natalie MacMaster, Mary Jane Lamond and the Mabou Dancers. The concert opened with tens of thousands of fallen autumn leaves—gathered up off the ground by volunteers—falling again from the ceiling of the erstwhile hockey rink, and a voice echoing in the darkness.

Frank Macdonald captured the moment in the *The Inverness Oran*: "The lights came up on the autumn colours of Natalie MacMaster's red dress and golden hair while her fiddle sang softly under the voice of the late Archie Neil Chisholm quoting poetry of his beloved Cape Breton Island: 'Wherever I roam, I'll never forget my Cape Breton home. Let others tell tales of the great golden west, but the land of my childhood is the land I love best. There are many large cities, that heaven may dome, but none can surpass you, my Cape Breton home.'

"John Allan Cameron then stepped to the podium to pay tribute to Archie Neil Chisholm, to whose memory the first annual Celtic Colours Music Festival was dedicated: 'Archie Neil's passion was the Celtic culture. He saw Cape Breton Island taking this culture and introducing it to the rest of the world. His dreams have become a reality. *Ciamar a tha sibh an nochd? Ciad Mile Fàilte.*'

"And a crowd of 3500 in Sydney's Centre 200 welcomed home

some of its best musicians, who brought along with them some of the best from the rest of the Celtic world."

Natalie MacMaster, the hugely popular fiddler from Troy, Inverness County, played host on this evening. Having local artists host the concerts was one of the planning details, welcoming visiting musicians and audience members to our Cape Breton communities. And Natalie played her role with the genuine down-home humility and charm she is known for all over the world.

"Are you guys ready yet?" she asked, and although she was checking with Cape Breton Gaelic singer Mary Jane Lamond and her band, who were setting up behind her, the audience responded heartily. Ready? Were they ever! And so were Mary Jane and her band, which included Creignish fiddler Wendy MacIsaac, Ray Montford (guitar), Geoff Arsenault (drums and percussion), John Diamond (bass), and Guy Turner (keyboards). Mary Jane—who had scored a hit with her vocal performance on "Sleepy Maggie" from Ashley MacIsaac's 1995 album, *hi$^{TM}$, how are you today?*— performed songs from her recently released album *Suas e!* Mary Jane's repertoire and arrangements showcased her love for and dedication to Cape Breton Island's Gaelic culture, while adding the contemporary touches that brought the music into the mainstream World Music category that was catching fire in the late 1990s. Although the sounds were inching towards the late twentieth century, the music was still set firmly in an earlier era, as Macdonald noted in the *Oran*: "At one point, Lamond turned to the audience, telling any visitors who might not be familiar with her music, 'I'm singing Gaelic. You're not losing your mind.'"

Opening with ancient Gaelic songs, which tradition says are at the root of Cape Breton-style Scottish music, it was only natural to follow with a dance—a component of Cape Breton's culture which many consider the basis for Cape Breton music's distinctive sound.

"The trademark of Cape Breton fiddle music is that its rhythms call out for people to dance to its music," wrote Macdonald, "and the Mabou Scotch Four demonstrated what that meant, stepping energetically to Wendy MacIsaac's fiddle and Joel Chiasson's piano."

Harvey MacKinnon of Whycocomagh leaped up next and wowed the crowd with a stepdancing solo. With arms deliberately lifeless at his sides, his intricate steps kept uncanny time to the tunes, giving the audience the added thrill of seeing the music brought vividly to life.

While the Cape Bretoners presented Gaelic song and local dance traditions during the first half, The Chieftains personified the program's promise of Cape Breton-Irish collaborations, showcasing the instrumental, vocal and dance styles of both traditions. Gerry Wright reported in *The Buzz*: "Sparkling their second half set with solos from practically everyone on stage, highlighted by Matt Molloy on flute and Sean Keane's fiddling." Tara Camus wrote that The Chieftains featured Irish dance champions Cara Butler and Donnie Golden and invited Mary Jane Lamond and Ashley MacIsaac on stage for a number. Ashley and Mary Jane had toured with The Chieftains, as had Natalie, so for the more informed in the audience, this collaboration may have been expected—except that Ashley wasn't scheduled to perform, and his surprise cameo brought 3500 people to their feet for a ten-minute ovation and a thundering encore for The Chieftains and their guests.

But perhaps the biggest surprise of the night may have been County Clare's Sharon Shannon on accordion. Shannon, a multi-instrumentalist whose parents were traditional dancers, absorbed an international cross-section of traditional music growing up in the "two-pub village" of Doolin, on Ireland's west coast. She was in the midst of recording her first album when a couple of fellows from Irish rock group The Waterboys heard her playing in a pub in County Galway and invited her to tour with them. After a year and a half on the road, Sharon returned to Galway, finished her album, and went on to set traditional music on its ear—not with gimmicks or a big show, just the contagious pure joy she exudes while making music. By Celtic Colours, Sharon had just released her third album, and although she had toured throughout the United Kingdom, Ireland, Australia, Europe and America, been featured in her own one-hour special on Irish television, and had a tune on the biggest selling Irish album of all time, *A Woman's Heart*, she was virtually unknown in Cape Breton. Local musician, record producer, and exceptional writer of liner notes—I don't know how else to introduce him—Paul MacDonald was there that night, one of the few who knew what this Cape Breton audience was in for. He wrote:

"She opened with a Paul Cranford tune, 'The Union Street Session,' named for Kyle MacNeil's legendary Union Street house-warming party a few years back. That tune would go on to be the hit of the festival. Everyone seemed to have a go at it—The Bumblebees, Natalie, The Barras, Máire O'Keeffe, Jerry Holland, and of course Mr. Cranford himself." That tune would also be recorded by Shannon and MacMaster during a session at Lakewind Sound Studios in Point Aconi and eventually included on the 2002 Celtic Colours compilation, *The Colours of Cape Breton*.

"At Centre 200, Sharon filled this reel with cascades of lyrical rolls and ornaments and created a sound of pure joy and lift. Her subtle improvisations seemed to fill the tune with life and energy. As Sharon navigated through this two-part tune, she still found room to fill out her sound with double-stops, left hand chords and rhythmic accents that always fit right into the harmonic rhythmic pocket set up by her accompanists. She followed 'Union Street' with a pair of traditional Irish dance reels.

"The accompaniment was simple, bass and guitar only, but spirited and rhythmic. Trevor Hutchinson (The Waterboys, Lúnasa) set the foundation on electric upright bass with his solid bass lines, drones and pedal points that drove the music into soaring crescendos. Donogh Hennessey's guitar playing is unique and unlike anything heard on Cape Breton before; powerfully rhythmic yet always complimentary to the phrasing and ornamentation of Sharon's playing. Also, his guitar playing was the perfect harmonic balance to Trevor's bass counterpoint. What a rhythm section: Trevor and Donogh! They really made the arrangement come to life. I think this first set of tunes left people wondering what they were hearing! The response was one of uncertainty."

Or maybe the crowd was simply stunned speechless—it's hard to say. Cape Breton audiences can be as blasé about traditional music as they can be openly impressed. It's sometimes hard to tell the difference. They also tend to be a highly knowledgeable crowd. This set—being unlike anything most had ever heard before—draws that fine line. The audience's true feeling would become obvious though.

Paul MacDonald went on: "After the second set, people had really warmed up to her music and a joyful mood carried the audience throughout the kaleidoscope of Celtic dance tunes. Sharon played through a repertoire that included Irish and Scottish, Portuguese, Québécois, American and more Cape Breton tunes including 'The Cottonwood Reel,' 'Mary Cottar's Jig' by Cranford, and 'The Trip to Windsor' by Dan R. MacDonald. A few sets of tunes on the fiddle illustrated that she is just as soulful and lyrical on the fiddle as she is on the button-box. By the time her performance reached its peak with a blistering set of Clare reels, learned from Tommy Peoples on the tin whistle, the audience was totally overwhelmed. The warmth and charm of her music had already brought many to their feet. Sharon finished with a Québécois fiddle tune I first heard many years ago at a rural house session north of Montreal. She interpreted this tune in an Irish dance style. Trevor and Donogh had fun and played on the tune's syncopated rhythmic structure and as they did, the arrangement gained dynamic momentum. The last eight bars were spectacular!"

Sharon Shannon had clearly made an impression on this audience.

"When she began to play, a hushed wonder filled the rink," said Sydney resident Bertha Ann MacLean, who was covering the concert for *What's Goin On* magazine. "All who heard this woman play her various accordions, her tin whistles—even the words she spoke seemed to have a musical rhyme to them. I think all who witnessed this Irishwoman wandered to their cars that October night never to forget Sharon Shannon's name. I never will."

Following The Chieftains and their ovations and encores,

Natalie MacMaster had the unenviable task of closing the four-and-a-half-hour concert. And, to no one's surprise, Natalie was up to the challenge, bringing the show home Cape Breton style. In sharp contrast with the high-stepping Irish dance style, Allan Hughie MacDonald of Judique kept his stepdancing close to the floor, and after an eight-hand reel by the Mabou Dancers, Natalie and her band—Dave MacIsaac on guitar, Joel Chiasson on piano, Bruce Jacobs on bass, and Tom Roach on drums—took over. Although the crowd was thinning towards the end of the second half, Natalie was in top form and delivered a number of selections from her 1996 Warner Music release *No Boundaries*. The music from this album stretched a little beyond the "traditional" Cape Breton idiom, but that didn't stop the die-hards in the crowd from dancing and clapping along to the energetically rendered music.

And then it was over, the first concert of the Celtic Colours International Festival. Despite a few criticisms—the concert went on too long, the sound was inadequate in places, there was too much down time between sets—the general consensus was that it had been a truly great night.

"This is worth every penny I paid for my ticket and much more," said Hilary MacNeil, who had traveled the hour and a half from Port Hawkesbury. "There is no place I'd rather be right now."

And who could blame her? To anyone who had any interest in or knowledge of this kind of music—this Celtic music that was making waves on the world-wide stage—it was clear that some of the best was coming from right here on the East Coast of Canada. And some of the most famous of its proponents were Cape Bretoners. It was proven during that first concert of Celtic Colours International Festival that our homegrown talent could hold their own with the world's best.

"I stood for a moment when I reached the damp air of the Sydney streets that night, the music still ringing in my ears," reflected Bertha Ann MacLean. "I wanted to remember this moment, this feeling. I felt such pride, as if I had played some part in the experience that left me feeling so satisfied, and sated. The clan I called home, my islanders, were somehow closer to me now, as if I shared in a piece of our culture, our history, our ability to shine. And we were brilliant."

## As Cape Bretoners, it's easy to get carried away by a sense of pride and ownership of this music and these musicians.

But the lure of this music extends beyond the shorelines and across the Canso Causeway. The *Cape Breton Post* reported that there were folks at the concert from Montana, Michigan, Oregon, Pennsylvania, Ontario and Newfoundland, many saying they were here especially to see The Chieftains. Big names had undoubtedly helped draw tourists and locals alike to this ambitious new event, but the real appeal in the design of Celtic Colours is in the bigger picture, not the bigger name acts. The impact of the festival is in the presentation of many top-quality acts scattered through tiny community halls that determined volunteers have built with their own hands and supported with dances and bake sales—not in the big opening concert at the biggest venue in the biggest town.

Now with one concert down and twenty-four to go, plus thirteen workshops scheduled for the next eight days, the festival must prove itself and justify the vision of its organizers and funders, including every person who bought a ticket to the promise of Celtic Colours.

"The opening show is an anomaly," said Joella Foulds in a 2004 interview. "We thought it would be nice to start off with something large—but we don't really like the large," she says, pointing out that like most of the concerts, the real life of the festival will be in the smaller communities, where concerts and workshops take place throughout the week in community, parish and fire halls, schools, theatres, a barn, a church and a ski lodge.

"Celtic Colours is different from most other large festivals," said Max MacDonald. "It has no single centre of activity. It is spread out in communities all over Cape Breton. It had to be that way. Cape Bretoners are enthusiastic participants in the traditional Gaelic-based culture. They pack the local halls to hear the fiddlers and dance the square sets. That's the way the culture is enjoyed and kept alive. So that's the way it will be presented for the Celtic Colours Festival."

A number of the concerts spread around the island in the festival's first year were designed to honour some of the island's most respected musicians. On Saturday night, "Winston's Classic Cuts" and "Peggy's Jig" paid tribute to two fiddlers who have had a pronounced influence on Cape Breton's fiddle music.

In Big Pond, on the Bras d'Or Lakes, "Winston's Classic Cuts" showcased players for whom Winston "Scotty" Fitzgerald was a hero, one of the most revered players in the Cape Breton tradition. Fitzgerald was a mid-twentieth-century superstar of the Cape Breton fiddle, with an uncanny ability to improve tunes with his embellishments. In the 1950s and '60s, Fitzgerald would be the first choice for dances, playing six nights a week all over the island with guitarist Estwood Davidson and piano player Beattie Wallace. His playing at dances and on radio broadcasts and records is often cited as a powerful influence among many of the next generation.

The concert was hosted by Carl MacKenzie, a well known dance player and composer from Washabuck, and featured Cape Breton fiddlers Jerry Holland, who as a child had literally looked up to Winston, sitting at his feet when Fitzgerald played at his parents' home in Boston in the 1950s; Brenda Stubbert, a prolific composer from the Northside; Jennifer Roland, who had inherited Winston's fiddle; and Queensville dance player and composer Dougie MacDonald. Doug MacPhee and Patricia Chafe provided the piano accompaniment, and Big Pond whiz kid Gordie Sampson repre-sented the local community with some songs and tunes on guitar. The line-up was rounded out by fiddlers Frank Ferrel and Joe

Cormier, visiting from the United States, and the big surprise of the opening concert, Sharon Shannon.

After a fourteen-hour drive from his home in New England, fiddler Frank Ferrel made it to Big Pond in time for the soundcheck Saturday afternoon. He remembers the scene as the show was about to get underway: "The Fire Hall was a lot smaller than I'd expected, set up in the traditional manner with tables crowded around a small dance floor, the bar open at one end, and the stage in the middle. Despite my misgivings, the estimated crowd that night was well over three hundred people. Each of us got twelve minutes or three sets of tunes. In some cases the three sets of tunes stretched to twenty minutes, what with the tendency on the part of Cape Breton fiddlers to play as many as twenty tunes in a set. By the time Dougie MacDonald got up to play, the crowd was sufficiently in their cups to find the prospect of staying seated just too much to bear. With Dougie's first note, most of the crowd bounded to the floor and began to dance. Dougie is a younger player, a dance player, and one of my favourites. There were still a number of performers left on the line-up when Dougie started his riot. Fiddler Carl MacKenzie was the emcee for the night and in a gesture of frustration, threw up his hands and was heard to comment, 'Well, so much for the concert, the crowd's running the show now!'"

The concert and dance went on until about one in the morning, and all of the scheduled performers got their chance to play. But that's the way it goes. Cape Breton fiddle music is music for dancing, and if the music is making you want to dance, you're gonna dance. And if the fiddler sees the crowd is wanting to dance, then there's gonna be a dance. I guess Frank Ferrel had never heard the expression, "I went to a concert and a dance broke out."

Across the island on the northeastern coast at Ski Cape Smokey Lodge in Ingonish, "Peggy's Jig" was dedicated to the late Ingonish fiddler Mike MacDougall. MacDougall was a fisherman who, like Fitzgerald, would adapt tunes to his own liking and in doing so would influence the playing of the next generation. He also had a unique repertoire that included local fiddle and pipe tunes and Irish songs and tunes, including his own "Peggy's Jig," which had caught on as a popular session tune throughout Ireland. Hosted by North Shore singer Buddy MacDonald—a fellow with deep roots because of his dad Tommy "Peggy," one of the revered North Shore Gaelic Singers—this concert included Mike's friend Gordon Côté, a Richmond County fiddler and piper, and Kevin Levesconte who accompanied him on guitar. Scottish piper Fred Morrison was there, in recognition of MacDougall's repertoire of pipe tunes. And the Irish were well represented by fiddler Máire O'Keeffe, dobro player Frankie Lane, Frankie's banjo-picking pal Éamonn Coyne, and those fun-loving Bumblebees.

While tribute was being paid posthumously to Winston "Scotty" Fitzgerald and Mike MacDougall, a living group from their era was reunited on that first Saturday night of Celtic Colours at the "MacLellan Trio Reunion" in Port Hawkesbury.

Theresa and Donald MacLellan were among the many Cape Breton fiddlers to cut their own 78 RPM's for the Celtic label in the 1940s and '50s. They were accompanied by their sister Marie on the piano. In later years they formed the MacLellan Trio and cut two LP's for the Celtic label. These albums became immediate classics and a selection from them is still available on CD. From the rural Richmond County community of Cleveland, these musicians carried on the traditions of their father, the legendary Big Ronald MacLellan.

The line-up for the evening crossed generations and included guitarist, fiddler, and encyclopedia of tunes Dave MacIsaac, accompanied on piano by Tracey Dares, and Gaelic fiddler Alex Francis MacKay of Kingsville with Washabuck pianist Gordon MacLean. Gordon has played with Carl and Hector MacKenzie and on MacKay's Rounder Records release called *A Lifelong Home*.

This concert not only reunited a classic Cape Breton trio, rooted in the old ways, the line-up also demonstrated a bridge of sorts, an example of how the music is living on, generation after generation after generation. It traced the music from the MacLellans' father, Big Ronald, who was said to have got his bow from the fairies, through to this trio of his children, and from the Old World tunes of Alex Francis MacKay—whose music, they say, was born from a local Gaelic culture and and then enriched by countless musicians, both local and itinerant—to Dave MacIsaac and Tracey Dares who released their first solo recordings in the 1990s. MacIsaac's 1995 *Nimble Fingers* won five East Coast Music Awards.

Over the years, this generational transmission would be encouraged by Celtic Colours programming. Enabling and celebrating the traditional aspects of the culture has been a conscious choice by the festival from the very beginning.

It was a curious and compelling mix of old and new during that first weekend of Celtic Colours in 1997. Saturday night's tributes and reunions gave way to Sunday traditions in community gatherings, craftsmanship, and music with a nod to both past and future.

"*Thoireamaid Taing,*" an ecumenical service held at St. Andrew's Church in Sydney, celebrated Thanksgiving in Gaelic with a massive choir assembled from Oranaiche Cheap Breatuinn, Comunn Seinn of Halifax, the St. Ann's Bay Gaelic Choir from the North Shore, the Antigonish Gaelic Choir, the Gaelic College Senior Choir, and the St. Columba Church Choir based in Iona. Demonstrations and displays at the Gaelic College in St. Ann's featured luthier Otis Tomas discussing the finer points of his craft and the local wood he uses to make fiddles, guitars, harps and mandolins for a variety of well-known Cape Breton musicians; world-renowned Scottish pipemaker Hamish Moore displaying some of his work; and an audio presentation of traditional Cape Breton music transferred from 78s to contemporary digital recordings by Paul MacDonald.

One concert in particular that weekend caught tradition in transmission—"Dance to the Piper" at the Gaelic College of Arts and Crafts in St. Ann's. It was dedicated to tradition-bearer Alex Currie, an eighty-seven-year-old piper from Frenchvale, Cape Breton County.

"Talk about standing room only," wrote Iain Kenneth MacLeod

in *What's Goin On* magazine. "I was wondering why they called this 'Dance to the Piper' if there was no room to dance! People were packed in like sardines to hear the likes of Barry Shears, Paul MacNeil, Jamie MacInnis, and Duncan and Fin Moore."

"Dance to the Piper"—which also featured John MacLean, Slainte Mhath's Bruce MacPhee, Pictou County native Scott Long from Ashley MacIsaac's band The Kitchen Devils, and two-time gold-medal-winning Scottish piper Fred Morrison—was named in honour of Alex Currie's older style, from the days when pipes were not thought of primarily as military instruments—when bagpipes meant dance. Pipers played for dancing in Cape Breton. That style of playing bagpipes goes back a long way, to the seventeenth century in Scotland, before the introduction of the violin, when "the bagpipe was the most prominent instrument in the Highlands and Islands." This concert represented a new generation's interest in this style of music, just when the idea of dancing to pipe music was in danger of being lost forever.

As time went on and the Gaelic way of life was being attacked in Scotland's Highlands and Islands, leading ultimately to the Clearances, Scottish fiddle music was redefined in the Lowlands and the role of bagpipes was given over to competition and regimented military exercises. But the old Gaelic dance style was still vibrant when they were clearing the land of people, so the traditional Gaelic style of playing bagpipes traveled with the players to their new land. As more and more left the Highlands and Islands and actions were taken to ban and burn the pipes, this traditional style of playing was all but lost in the Old Country. But in Cape Breton, where many settled, the tradition continued.

The concert's host, Barry Shears, had written in his 1995 book, *The Cape Breton Collection of Bagpipe Music*, "They brought with them bagpipes, fiddles, and a strong dance tradition. The first immigrant pipers were Gaelic speakers. Unable to read or write music, they transmitted tunes orally. The role of the piper was essentially that of a folk musician. While he performed at a variety of social gatherings, from weddings to wakes, the true test of the skill of a piper was whether he could play for stepdancers. In order to play for dances, a piper required a vast repertoire of music. He would have to play for three to four hours for dancers, without written music. Also a piper needed to master the difficult timing and rhythm technique necessary for stepdancing."

By the late twentieth century, however, due to the pressures of industrialization and modernization and the emphasis on military bands and competitions, this unique style of piping was on its way to the history books as few of the pioneer players' descendants were carrying on this dance tradition.

"By the 1930s, many of the old pipers were dying, and the speedy transition from piping as an expression of a folk culture to a purely competitive form had begun. The ability to play for solo and group stepdancing, once the measure of a piper's skill in Cape Breton, was being lost. So compelling was the drive to produce competitive pipers that the art of dance playing had all but vanished.

"Despite this wave of competitive and rigidly uniform playing standards, there remained in Cape Breton isolated pockets of pipers trained in the much older 'oral' tradition. These players were part of a parallel piping culture. They retained their individual style of playing the old tunes and the ability to play for stepdancers. Their playing did not conform with the Army or competition style. Instead of being acknowledged and appreciated as exponents of a folk culture, their style of playing was considered inferior and viewed as an anomaly to be corrected. Ridiculed by some pipers at home and from Scotland, they found themselves pressured into learning the twentieth-century style.

"Just as the bagpipe had usurped the harp in seventeenth-century Scotland, so too would it fall victim to the popularity and range of the violin in late-twentieth-century Cape Breton. The traditional Cape Breton piper has all but passed into history, replaced by pipe bands and a competition-oriented culture which values uniformity and technique over music style and expression."

But when Alex Currie was growing up in rural Cape Breton,

the old way was still very much alive. Having learned the tunes orally from his mother, whose family left South Uist for Cape Breton in the 1800s, "his music represents an undiluted oral Gaelic tradition reaching back to nineteenth-century Scotland. He didn't have a set scale but instead learned to lift certain fingers to reproduce the sound he wanted. Alex's style of playing was developed at a time when the bagpipes were used for social dances. He almost invariably performs sitting down, beating time with the rhythmic action of both feet, a scene common in some parts of Cape Breton over forty years ago. His repertoire consists mostly of dance music, jigs, strathspeys, and reels and his performance on the pipes must surely be a glimpse of what one would have found in the South Uist of two hundred years ago."

Currie told Ronald Caplan in 1997: "When I was seventeen or eighteen . . . pipes were more common than the violin. You go to a party, the old people wanted the old music, you know. It was dancing, and stepdancing. My sister and my brothers, my mother and father, were good dancers, too." Alex learned to play the pipes from his older brother. He got his tunes from his mother, and his father, who'd "play a little bit," showed him how to make a chanter.

"I play a different style," explains Currie. "I play the old-style music. And that came from Scotland 300 years ago, over here. That's the style I've got. They're crazy about it. From Scotland, they all come over, see what the hell is going on, see what kind of a piper I am.

"I played it the same as I was brought up with. And I'm proud of that today because they appreciate it today, the pipers. Because they haven't got the style I've got, and they come here from all over the world, pretty near all over the world, the last five years, trying to get that . . . . Every day. Hear a lot about it, you know. And they hear a lot about Alex Currie."

Scottish pipe-maker and player Hamish Moore made a tape of Currie playing in Cape Breton in the early 1970s. One of the people who heard it was Fred Morrison.

From the stage during the "Dance to the Piper" concert, Fred

Morrison said: "When Hamish had been out, like, checking out the music in Cape Breton and all the rest of it, he met the legendary Alex Currie, and he came back and he gave me a tape of Alex and a lot of your old fiddle players and all that, you know. And just the rhythm and the feel of all the music revolutionized my musical career and feel for the music so that's really a great honour for me to be playing here in the presence of Alex Currie and all the rest of it. So thank you."

This would be the first time Fred Morrison and Alex Currie met—and what a meeting it turned out to be.

Currie remembered: "So this Morrison—I never met him till that night. Seumas Moore had a tape I made over here in '73. And he always carries it with him. So he played it for Morrison over in the Old Country. Nothing to do, he had to come over to see me. So when he saw me over here: 'I have to congratulate you,' he says. 'You're a great piper.' Well, I didn't know who I was talking to. He said, 'I came over with Seumas Moore to hear you.' 'Well, that's good,' I said. 'You're not going to hear me play the pipes, but I'll play a tune on the chanter.'

"I couldn't blow the pipes. So we turned the chanter. My nephew, Johnny MacLean—he turned the chanter in the pipes for me. And I got up on the stage—everybody in the place roared! They saw me playing the pipes, or playing the chanter, you know.

"So when I was done the chanter, he came over again. He said, 'I've got to congratulate you again. That was wonderful.' But I couldn't play the damn pipes, you know—I'm old—didn't have the wind. Johnny MacLean, my nephew, he got the bag going. Oh, Morrison got a hell of a surprise. And he's a gold-medal winner—two-gold-medalist.

"Then he got up on stage, he played. Well, I heard pipers, I heard pipers. And I never heard the like of that. He was something out of the world altogether. You'd think he was learned by the fairies, you know. He could do anything with them—with his fingers."

It was a great show—a great blast of pipes. Jamie MacInnis of

Big Pond and Paul MacNeil of Barra Glen were there, of whom Michael Grey had written, "There are few people in the world who equal Jamie and Paul in their presentation of the fine old music." Alex Currie's nephew John MacLean performed. Hamish Moore's sons Duncan and Fin, Pictou County Piper Scott Long. Iain Kenneth MacLeod wrote that "Slainte Mhath's Bruce MacPhee got to strut his stuff on the pipes with a drivin' version of 'Brucie & the Troopers.'

"Fred Morrison capped off the show with what appeared to be magic. He made it look easy. When it was over, I could not believe how diverse and eclectic an entire show dedicated to bagpipes could sound, but with the introduction of the border pipes, the A pipes, and the Scottish Small Pipes, it was an afternoon to remember."

And Alex Currie was there, sitting in the audience with Hamish Moore: "Well, Lord," he said after, "honest to God, boy—what a gang! You never heard the like. There was about twenty pipers all together. And stepdancers. Whale of a time. I was just there looking at the thing. Had me there as a—it was a gift to me, you know. It was a hell of a good time. They had 240 tickets and they sold out in no time."

Rita and Mary Rankin lent their voices to a taping of CBC radio's popular regional show *Atlantic Airwaves* at Cape Breton University's Boardmore Playhouse. *What's Goin On* reported: "Behind them were the Halifax-based MacCrimmon's Revenge, whom I'd heard some great things about and was eager to see for myself. To my surprise, they were not 'just another Celtic pub band'; they were much deeper and somewhat ethereal. They played traditional tunes on the small pipes, but the typical driving rhythm I associate with such reels and jigs was replaced by layer upon layer of drones and meditative percussion. It was extremely interesting and trance-inducing. Cello, guitar, bodhran, low whistle and didgeridoo gave them a pretty distinctive sound and their own place in the festival. Following a short break, the audience was treated to a true Cape Breton kitchen session with Dave MacIsaac, Jerry Holland, Gordon

Côté, and Carl MacKenzie on a forest of fiddles and Dougie MacPhee and Mary Jessie Gillis taking turns on the ivories. The fiddlers took turns playing some of their own favourite selections and, at the end, they all played in unison. After a well-deserved encore . . . each fiddler took turns deciding which way the arrangement would be heading in a true example of cooperative competition!"

"The Cape Breton Keyboard" concert was dedicated to the memory of well-known Cape Breton pianist Margaret MacPhee, who had passed away earlier that year.

"I was looking forward to this night in order to see the stage covered in ebony and ivory," wrote MacLeod. "Actually, from where I was sitting, I thought the night should have been sponsored by Roland keyboards! Tracey Dares was the host. Ryan MacNeil, Margaret's son Doug MacPhee, Patricia Chafe, George MacInnis and Maybelle Chisholm MacQueen were all given the opportunity to play some of their own choice cuts, and each player demonstrated a rather different perspective on the instrument. Emotion overflowed George MacInnis with every key he touched. Maybelle Chisholm MacQueen had all kinds of tricks up her sleeve as she danced up and down the keyboard, creating a blur of red nail polish. Pat Chafe played a couple of the many many pieces she has written. Ryan MacNeil gave the grand piano a good working over with his groove-laden style. And Doug MacPhee seemed to sit effortlessly at the bench and play in his own legendary way. If that wasn't enough, we also witnessed various pairings, most memorably Dougie and George and Tracey. Hearing three generations of accompaniment truly took the cake . . . ."

Thursday's "Highland Guitar Summit" in Judique brought together the "cream of the crop"—Celtic guitar players from Cape Breton, Nova Scotia, Ireland and England hosted by John Allan Cameron. And the "Northside Irish" concert on Friday in Englishtown focused on a style of music influenced by Ireland, but with Cape Breton twists. Hosted by fiddler Paul Cranford, this concert included the Barra MacNeils and many Northside players influenced by the Irish repertoire of Cape Breton's Henry Fortune, Joe Confiant and Johnny Wilmot. The Christmas Island Féis committee and a host of local Gaelic singers welcomed visiting Scottish Gaelic singers to their "Traditional Cape Breton Gaelic Evening" workshop and milling frolic. And the Mabou Féis brought pipers and Gaelic singers from Scotland to their opening weekend workshops and concert, which included over thirty local performers.

**Quietly, and almost always in the background, the small communities and their valiant volunteers are the bedrock of the success of Celtic Colours.**

In the beginning, Celtic Colours put out a call inviting community groups to meet with festival organizers to talk about the concept of an international Celtic festival. "Later, ads were placed in all the Cape Breton newspapers for expressions of interest. The response was overwhelming—so much so that the number of community events ended up being almost double what was projected. The Board of Directors for the Celtic Colours Festival Society set the criteria that hosting groups be non-profit organizations. There were plenty who fit the bill and who had a history of holding concerts, square dances, ceilidhs or Gaelic festivals.

"The role of the hosting communities varies. In all cases, it involves many volunteers at the local level and an opportunity for the groups to make some money for their own projects and draw attention to the work they do. Organizations such as the Inverary Manor will raise money toward the purchase of a van for residents of the Manor. The Chestico Museum and Historical Society will bring focus to their annual stepdancing festival. The Green Door Workshop in Chéticamp will raise some much-needed funds and bring world-class artists to their community. Féis an Eilein in Christmas Island had very specific ideas for their event, which supported their work in preserving Gaelic songs and language. Féis Mhàbu brought their fifth annual Féis into the festival along with the very successful Mabou Annual Thanksgiving Concert. While they receive some financial help from Celtic Colours and some visiting artists, they will conduct their event in the way they always do. The only difference may be that visiting audiences get to see what Mabou does so well. Every community has its own story and its own reasons for wanting to be involved.

"Communities are in the final stages of preparation for their hosting role—holding meetings to assign volunteer tasks, putting up posters and distributing brochures, selling tickets, deciding who will set up the hall and who will prepare the food for the performers."

Along with the music, a lot of people carry away the memory of the community meals—the finest meal you could not get in any restaurant in North America. These are prepared and hosted by volunteers in—frankly, you name the community! These are people who were up all night cooking and setting up the tables, are there at the door to greet you, make sure you have another cup of hot tea, send you away with tea biscuits and squares, then stay into the wee hours taking down staging, putting away the chairs, washing the floors and dishes, and leaving the hall spotless for the next community event.

As with any substantial cultural venture in a land of scarce funding, there were those who grumbled about support going to Celtic Colours instead of, as they read it, promoting Gaelic language and culture. *Oran* newspaper reporter Frank Macdonald took on the issue directly and with some force. He wrote:

"The festival was not without its critics, or more precisely, the funding for the festival was not without its critics. Some people involved in efforts to keep the Gaelic culture alive in Cape Breton through a re-birth of its fading language felt that the funding could have been better spent in education programs that would inform and/or teach the language to students."

Macdonald pointed out that "the festival itself can offer an excellent opportunity for the Gaelic community to inform the world of its concern that hundreds of millions of dollars are earned through tourism in this province by marketing the Gaelic culture around the world, while not a dime is re-invested in the preservation and promotion of the language that is largely responsible for the bonanza . . . . It is not too much to ask that a tiny portion of the revenues be used to prime the pump through school programs that introduce children to a language that some may choose to pursue to fluency."

Frank might have added that Celtic Colours had a School Program in place from the beginning, featuring Festival artists going into the schools, as well as workshops in Gaelic language and song at Féis Mhàbu, a Gaelic trade show with exhibits from various organizations, institutions and businesses involved in the Gaelic arts and culture, and an ecumenical Thanksgiving church service featuring six Gaelic choirs. And this commitment to the language grew through the years, eventually inviting Mary Jane Lamond as Artist in Residence. During her term, as well as perform, she advised the organizers on Gaelic content in the festival, and helped put together some of the concert line-ups.

Volunteers are an essential core to the success of Celtic Colours. The work is enjoyable—but volunteers also eliminate the expense of additional staff. They get to show off their community and possibly bring in a few dollars, but that can't be much compared to what they give to make the whole thing work. Without volunteers some festival ventures would never get off the ground. Carsden from Tønder Festival in Denmark told me his festival, which has been on the go for over twenty years, manages with one employee and thousands of volunteers. That's not quite the ratio here. While tapping into the volunteer spirit, Celtic Colours also has to create jobs. Jobs get essential work done. You can't rely only on the good-will of others or the government for assistance forever.

The world today knows that Celtic Colours flourished, but back in 1998 reporter Parker Donham referred to its "quirky, counter-intuitive economics." No one in print handled the realities of those economics better than Donham. He set the scene—"picture a fog-shrouded evening in Ingonish"—and then he described the show:

"Any of the four acts playing Ski Cape Smokey Lodge that Wednesday night—Archie Fisher, a renowned Scottish folk singer reminiscent of Pete Seeger; Anita Best, a founding vocalist with Figgy Duff whose work preserving Newfoundland culture has made her a national treasure; Eleanor Shanley, a high-octane Irish singer whose incandescent voice electrified the festival; and Bernard Felix and Norman Fromanger, a delightful button accordion-electric base duo from the French-descended community around The Rock's Port-au-Port Peninsula—could have captivated the audience single-handedly."

But for the one ticket price—ten dollars—the audience enjoyed performances by all four.

Then Parker did the math and described the remarkable setting. A sold-out crowd, and none of the 220 seats was more than 50 feet from the stage. That meant a gate of "just $2,200 to pay seven first-rate folk musicians—three of whom, counting Shanley's guitarist, had crossed the Atlantic to be there."

Of course, being Celtic Colours, the Ingonish event was only one of several scheduled around Cape Breton on that one night. At the same moment, some of the world's finest bagpipers, fiddlers and singers were performing under the festival's banner in equally small communities and venues such as the Christmas Island Fire Hall, Port Hood Consolidated School and the Glendale Parish Hall.

And of course this was only one night of a nine-day festival. And that was when the festival was much smaller. "Twelve thousand people attended 32 concerts at 26 different venues."

And then there was the Festival Club—to some people the very heart and potentially most creative and magical venue of Celtic Colours. For "nine nights running, the public could pay $5 to hear the best Celtic musicians in the world improvising 'til dawn." And it was located not in Sydney with a population of 27,000 but in the village of Baddeck—population of about 1,500.

"Last year," Parker wrote, "Celtic Colours made its headquarters in Sydney, but in what will rank as the dumbest marketing decision of the year, the Delta Sydney this year declined to offer any discount on the roughly $100,000 worth of hotel rooms the festival purchases.

So organizers switched the base camp to the more centrally located Baddeck. 'They may have been the only game in town,' said organizer Max MacDonald, 'but they weren't the only town in town.'"

And then Parker underlined the quirky economics of it all: The move from Sydney to Baddeck had "the unexpected result of boosting Festival Club attendance from 100-150 a night in Sydney to 200-300 in Baddeck. Go figure."

The article went on to point out that there was more to Celtic Colours than just the performances. There were workshops in every subject from square dancing to the Gaelic language, "art exhibits, milling frolics,…and banquets that took place throughout the week." And all of this had to have a cost.

Then there were programs in the public schools: "Celtic Colours in the Schools" saw Gaelic singer Jeff MacDonald (Goiridh Dòmhnallach) and young Cape Breton fiddlers Mac Morin, Mairi Rankin and Lisa MacIsaac give more than thirty free performances around the island.

And here's the kicker: "Run by a nonprofit society, the festival, now in its second year, gets about one-third of its $700,000 budget from ticket sales and concessions, a third from corporate sponsors (including critically important musicians' plane flights from Air Nova), and a third from the federal-provincial 'Years of Music' program. (That's a fraction of what the Nova Scotia Tattoo gets, more than a decade after organizers promised to wean it off government subsidies.)"

The point—or one point of many—is this: In 1998 Celtic Colours certainly looked fragile. It seemed to be loved by nearly everyone the festival touched—brought thousands to the island and extended the tourist season by over a week and, eventually, would pour millions of new dollars into the Cape Breton economy year after year—and yet it had no reliable economic footing, not even a fair amount of guaranteed government support.

"That year the Nova Scotia 'Years of Music' program came to an end. Officials of the departments of Education and Culture, and

Economic Development and Tourism, are considering a festival proposal for five years of declining assistance, at the end of which, Celtic Colours would be self-supporting."

All organizer Joella Foulds could offer was this: "At this time, we don't know if there will be a festival next year."

Let's face it, I can't help but sound like one terrific ad! European acts wheedle and cajole organizers for an invitation to play Celtic Colours. And people from around the world plan their vacations so that they can be in Cape Breton in October.

Ultramar was a sponsor, giving a fuel discount printed on the back of concert ticket stubs. And the car rental agencies—Budget and National Car—gave a discount to festival-goers if they used a promotion code.

But probably as important as those discounts was the determined cooperation of people like Lou Leith. Gordie Campbell tells this story: "Shetlanders Davie Henderson and Davie Gardner showed up one year as part of the festival's ongoing association with international festival presenters, arts organizations and media, and I told them: 'Don't worry when you get here. We'll take you to the concerts.'

"So they were driven to the concerts and Festival Club and stuff like that. And there was no bus at that point, no shuttles going back and forth to Baddeck, so there were a lot of demands for the drivers very late at night. So they said they wanted to rent a car.

"And at this point we were using an agency in Sydney and the woman that represented them was a lovely woman named Lou Leith, a star for many years in the background, and when she changed companies she took the sponsorship of the festival with her and she did an amazing job of taking care of the festival. But that year she only had certain cars available—things like a red mustang convertible 5.0. So Davie and Davie asked to get a car. I phoned Lou up, and Lou said, 'Well I don't have one.' And I said, 'Well what do you have?' And she said, 'I have a Lincoln

Continental.' And she made it available to us at a very good rate. And I didn't tell Davie and Davie.

"And in Britain, in Scotland certainly, the cars are very small. So they went into Sydney to pick up this car. And they just couldn't believe the size of it. They were like kids at Christmas, their eyes were this big. And they arrived back at the Gaelic College and they were like, 'What did you dooo?' They'd never seen anything that size in their lives. It was twice the size of a car they'd normally drive. Davie Gardner could actually sleep across the back seat and never touch the doors on each end.

"So then, they just proceeded to make that into their own personal party mobile. And I had to explain the licensing laws in regard to drink in cars and stuff, because it's very different—they safely and respectfully obeyed them of course. No sense getting jammed up in a foreign country for something, even if it is perfectly legal and acceptable at home. So they had a trunk full of beer. And the trunk was huge. And a video was made, one of the most memorable videos. Phil Cunningham and Tony McManus were there that year. Davie Henderson driving away, Davie Gardner filming, Phil Cunningham and Tony McManus sitting in the boot of the car having a little session, sitting in the trunk of the car playing accordion and guitar, just having a little session—as staff and artists watched from the parking lot side steps of MacLeod House. It was a glorious afternoon and just the right time for some artist-driven shenanigans."

As the festival was wrapping up toward the end of the week, I pulled a rare early-morning assignment, to drive a group called Waterson:Carthy from Festival headquarters, the Holiday Inn, to the Sydney airport. Waterson:Carthy was guitarist Martin Carthy, singer Norma Waterson, and singer/fiddler Eliza Carthy. Waterson:Carthy, whom I'd never heard of, is typical of the type of act that Celtic Colours would book—unknown to most, but revered by those who knew them.

Martin Carthy has been called one of the 100 greatest guitarists of the twentieth century by *Musician Magazine,* and when I was offering assignments to writers and photographers for *What's Goin On*, Dougie Johnson—a mean guitar-player himself and a talented photographer to boot—jumped at the chance to cover any show involving one of his heroes, Martin Carthy. Johnson covered "Whycocomagh Gathering," which featured the Eskasoni Fiddlers, Leahy, Pamela Morgan and Waterson:Carthy.

Johnson arrived late and couldn't find a parking space near the Whycocomagh Consolidated School. He managed to get himself situated by the soundboard just in time for the master of ceremonies, Celtic Colours board member and Whycocomagh impresario Burton MacIntyre, to introduce the show. The first half scheduled the Eskasoni Fiddlers—Wilfred Prosper, George Paul, and Paul Wukitsch; Pamela Morgan—a folk singer-songwriter from Newfoundland who once sang with the popular group Figgy Duff; and Waterson:Carthy—the reason Johnson took the assignment. Ontario-based family group Leahy was to perform during the second half of the show.

Johnson was looking forward particularly to the third act of the evening, but he enjoyed the first two acts just fine, describing the Eskasoni Fiddlers as playing "a set of very traditional sounding Cape Breton fiddle music . . . in a relaxed sort of way—meat and potatoes with no glitter and no jive—an excellent beginning." He was also generous in his praise of Morgan who was accompanied by her brother George on piano and Russian violinist Sergei Tchepournov. "Her voice is haunting and dark, perfect for the moody music she sings. You're not going to get up and dance to this music, you're going to surrender to its dreamy, trance-like effect."

But it's Waterson:Carthy that Johnson had come to see, and they were up next.

Johnson wrote: "Now a young lady with neon green hair walks onto the stage, places two fiddles by a microphone and stands around looking a bit lost. The kilted emcee tells us that Martin Carthy and Norma Waterson are unfortunately stuck in Toronto and will not make the gig . . . . So, I'm disappointed. As it turns out, the green-haired lass is their daughter Eliza, the third member of Waterson:Carthy, and she is going to perform solo. At once she endears herself to the crowd. Being alone among strangers on her first day in Canada, she feels a little like a fish out of water. She frankly states: 'I miss me mum!'

"Eliza starts with an a cappella English folk song—a strange twisted melody and lyrics from another century when the world was a far different place and people lived closer to the elements. This material has the inherent danger of being academic and irrelevant. But her beautiful, eerie performance touches on human emotions and situations that are universal and know no sense of time. My disappointment is gone. She is working the same rich vein of English folk music mined by her parents, whose careers date back to the early sixties.

"One of the fiddles she plays has an altered tuning which she uses to accompany another song. Again this droning fiddle pumping behind another set of archaic lyrics is a touchstone to a shared pre-history. Judging by the enthusiastic audience response I was not the only one moved by this talented individual."

I missed that show, but I would discover Eliza Carthy again years later when Irish songwriter Billy Bragg was involved in a project recording some of Woody Guthrie's lost songs. Eliza played fiddle on those tracks. On discovering this in the liner notes of *Mermaid Avenue: The Complete Sessions*, I had what would become a strangely familiar feeling in subsequent years, one of those "I know who that is" moments. She indeed carries the family tradition to the next generation. Since then I have seen her perform at Glasgow's Celtic Connections with Sharon Shannon and others.

But back to Dougie Johnson. He finally got to see his guitar hero Martin Carthy a couple of nights later in Judique at the "Highland Guitar Summit." This concert also featured Cape Breton trailblazer John Allan Cameron, the man who was out there ahead of us all, years before, playing fiddle tunes on his twelve-string guitar, in his kilt on the stage of the Grand Old Opry. Also featured was Halifax's Dave MacIsaac, who plays as if his musical soul was born on Cape Breton Island two hundred years ago but grew up via the Deep South and the Mississippi Delta; the flamboyantly mesmerizing Irish slide guitar player Frankie Lane; Cape Bretoners J.P. Cormier and Gordie Sampson; and André Marchand from Québec, who said he was a little awed by his stage mates, telling the audience that his music was influenced by some of the players on that stage.

"Finally I got to hear Martin Carthy live," wrote Johnson, greatly relieved. "I was always intrigued by his percussive guitar style and his staccato vocals. His guitar is weirdly tuned—C-G-C-D-G-A—so there is no one else who sounds like him. A large part of his repertoire consists of Morris dance tunes, so the audience is hearing something unfamiliar. Second time round, he sang and played an English folk song."

Johnson may not have seen as much of Martin Carthy as he would have liked but, as noted in Frank Macdonald's account for *The Inverness Oran*, the guitarist's presence was certainly felt at Celtic Colours: "Martin Carthy performed a song, 'Deserter.' As the concert closed, the famous English performer had to pack up his guitar quickly and catch a flight to Chicago where he was playing the following night. But his presence in Judique drew fans from as far away as Sydney to hear him because Carthy had missed his performance in Whycocomagh. He was flight-fouled and didn't arrive. He was worth both trips just to hear him once, according to one Glace Bay guitarist." Did I mention that Dougie Johnson is from Glace Bay?

I got to see Waterson:Carthy—all three of them—during a "Louisbourg Crossroads" concert at the Louisbourg Playhouse, a building left over from the set of the Walt Disney movie *Squanto* when it was filmed in Cape Breton. It was turned into a theatre venue by the community. The Louisbourg Playhouse Society took over the structure and upgraded it to withstand weather and to include modern creature comforts, and they had been running summer concert series ever since. I had driven the Bumblebees who shared the bill with Waterson:Carthy; the Québécois trio of André Marchand, Lisa Ornstein and Normand Miron; and Cape Bretoners Shawn MacDonald on fiddle and Doug MacPhee on piano. As a group, Waterson:Carthy tended to weave melody and harmony in overlapping waves of voice and instrument. I liked this effect, especially how it moved around, and found myself humming a tune from memory in the bathroom during intermission.

Days later, I had to drive Waterson:Carthy to the Sydney airport. To complicate matters, beyond the fact that it was very early in the morning, keys to one of the rentals had been misplaced and the only other vehicle available was a cargo van with no seats in it. They had to get to the airport to catch their departing flights in time to make a connection in Halifax to get to Chicago for a gig that night, so I did what had to be done and volunteered the car I had been driving—a four-door Honda Accord belonging to my girlfriend—ill-suited though it was for the mission.

It presented me with a designated-driver problem: I had three people and their gear to fit into a four-door car. Martin had a couple of guitars, Eliza had her fiddle, and each one had luggage suitable for transatlantic travel. The trunk filled up first with some, but not all, of the luggage. The instruments, except for the fiddle, wouldn't fit in the trunk, being housed in oversized airline safe cases. We carefully orchestrated the load in. First we belted Martin into the front seat and arranged various bits and pieces of luggage and instrument cases around his legs and on his lap. Then we filled the back seat, arranging the rest of the luggage around Eliza and Norma. It wasn't the most comfortable trip, but we had all squeezed in and made it happen, and this is what being a driver for the festival is all about: making the most of a situation that seems impossible, a little give here, a little take there, and mission accomplished in the end. It wasn't luxurious, but they all appreciated the extra effort. And we laughed and joked about it the whole way to the airport.

"Louisbourg Crossroads" host Ken Donovan tried to tie the Irish, French, Scottish, and English history of Louisbourg together in an effort to justify the apparently eccentric program. He was helped a lot as the music told its own story. The story turned out to be about the tunes. I'm sure many in the audience familiar with Cape Breton-style tunes—which tend to be of Scottish, Irish, or Cape Breton origin—noticed the similarities and differences in repertoire and construction.

Shawn MacDonald and Doug MacPhee played a tasty selection of familiar tunes recognizable across Cape Breton. Shawn's showpiece "The Hangman" is always impressive—especially when introduced with a story—and Doug is immaculate on the keys.

The set by the André Marchand Trio—André Marchand on guitar, vocals and feet, classically-trained violinist and traditional musicologist Lisa Ornstein, and funny guy singer and button accordionist Normand Miron—was especially interesting for its devotion to French Canadian folklore, and for Marchand's unusual accompaniment, using his feet as an additional rhythm instrument.

Regardless of the historical significance of the venue, I wanted to hear the contemporary Bumblebees: Liz Doherty (fiddle), Laoise Kelly (harp and fiddle), Mary Shannon (banjo, fiddle and bouzouki), and Colette O'Leary (piano accordion). They played an impressive diversity of tunes—from Cape Breton, Ireland, Denmark, Québec, Scotland—and their diversity of instruments made for an infinitely entertaining set. They were there for the music and, having an André Marchand tune in their vast repertoire, sat on the floor in front of the stage for Marchand/Ornstein/Miron's entire set. A couple of Irish steps and a tune with Mary Shannon and the night was complete. And the crowd had enough stamina left to be on its feet.

And while folks around the island were buying up CDs and heading for the Festival Club and house parties, my last assignment that year was driving a well-known, platinum-selling Scottish group to the airport, just before noon the day after they had celebrated their last night at the festival. It was shaping up to be a sketchy day all around, after not nearly enough sleep and a little more-than-enough partying. Luckily, I was driving, not them, and they were definitely in need of something to dull the self-inflicted pain. Of course, I didn't really know what was going on as they chatted among themselves in the van. It's not a long drive from downtown Sydney to the Sydney airport, but it took most of the ride for me to figure out what these guys were saying. Even after a week, I hadn't quite gotten the hang of translating from Scottish-accented English to Cape Bretonese in real time. But growing up in Cape Breton, and having spent quality time with Newfoundlanders, I was catching on to local dialects and accents in English and the slang that these subtle differences produce.

Actually, it's funny how quickly you can pick up an accent when you spend an intense period of time surrounded by it. You find its inflections showing up in your own speech, and you simply find yourself following more of the conversation around you. In some ways their speech—and by their I mean those who speak the varieties of English from Ireland, Scotland, and England—is more familiar, more like the way people around here talk, with their regionally recognizable vernacular and the different "grace notes" from place to place. I can usually tell if someone's from North Sydney/Sydney Mines, New Waterford, Glace Bay, Mabou or Whitney Pier just by "tawkin' t'dem."

So it took me most of the ride out to the airport to realize what my shotgun-riding passenger meant when he was asking if it was okay to "skin up" in the van. And it kind of surprised me. I knew my rock-and-roll, but up to that point, I don't think I got it that so-called "Celtic" musicians could be so hip that they'd be into that kind of thing. I guess the idea of Celtic music that I had was that it's traditional music, and the implication is that traditional music is old music played by old people, especially if you are on the outskirts of that tradition—as I was. I'm sure I'm forgetting that the old were once very young. Because, in the wider sense of things, and from a U.K./European perspective, this music is folk music, and Celtic Colours is a music festival. And this is the kind of thing that goes on at music festivals and among all musicians. I thought of my own generation, and it wasn't hard to imagine some of them partying like "rock stars," but I had a hard time picturing Theresa, Marie and Donald MacLellan, Buddy MacMaster, Alex Francis MacKay or Carl MacKenzie sneaking out behind the hall between sets and "skinning up."

# The first Festival Club at Celtic Colours was in the basement of the Holiday Inn in Sydney.

It was held in the multi-purpose meeting rooms with all the sliding doors open except for one section, behind the stage. This area served as the Green Room. This is the warm-up and cool-down area where musicians gather to sort out tunes together and generally hang out, before they go onstage to play for the Festival Club audience. There was a cash bar for the public near the stage, but back in the Green Room the beer flowed freely, delivered in six-packs from a seemingly endless supply. Before long, there were more than just the performers backstage. Volunteers and "chancers" started to make their way back, whether legitimately looking for someone or hopefully hanging on to someone else—whatever would work to get them closer to the music and to hanging out with the musicians.

Usually, when musicians are playing a gig, in bars especially, by the time they are finished playing the bar is closed. So when they go looking for a drink to unwind and socialize after work, it sometimes can be hard to find a place. And that's where the Celtic Colours Festival Club comes in. That the organizers set it up conveniently in the host hotel is all the better, as it's only a short trip back to your room at the end of the night.

The Club is set up so that when the artists arrive back at the communal residence after their island-wide performances, they have a place to relax, have a few drinks and catch up with the other performers. And as it's all music anyway, artists are invited to take a turn on the Club's stage—a chance to play, and play together, in a setting more comfortable than the formal concerts. The Club is open to the public for an admission fee which is discounted if you present your ticket stub from one of that day's concerts. Festival-goers grab at this rare chance to see the stars. There is a stage set up, but the informal atmosphere makes it seem much more intimate than a concert.

And the real action isn't always on stage. Often it's in the Green Room, where the musicians are playing just for themselves and other musicians gather around them to listen and learn. This isn't performing, just playing and sharing songs and stories, because this often is one of the places the culture lives and breathes, gets encouragement and new life. I think this kind of gathering is the heart and soul of the festival.

Visiting Irish accordionist Sharon Shannon watches closely as Cape Breton's "First Lady of the Violin," Winnie Chafe, plays a warm-up tune in the Green Room. She takes the chance to question Chafe about different parts and softly plays along, a mini cassette recorder running between them. Fred Morrison is sitting beside Scottish Gaelic singers Ishbel MacAskill, Mairi Smith and Cathy-Ann MacPhee—the former from the Isle of Lewis, the latter from the Isle of Barra, since relocated to Canada—as they sing unaccompanied, taking turns with the Gaelic lyrics.

"These women are Goddesses," Fred half jokes. "In Scotland it's very rare indeed to see them all together."

And while all of this goes on, musicians are called out to go on stage to play to the waiting audience. The audience knows this is a bonus. Most of them have already been to a concert this evening, somewhere in Cape Breton. You pretty well knew who you would see. But at the Festival Club, the crowd enjoys one another, perhaps gets a few words with a musician they admire—and since this is an atmosphere where anything can happen, any mix of musicians is liable to perform.

But out there, it's not the same as in the Green Room. It's back to performer and audience. Of course the paying audience gets a good show—these are, after all, topnotch professional musicians— but what is different in the Green Room is that more intimate exchange between artists; a head cocked to one side, eyes intent on the fingering, a quick flash of eureka when someone sees, finally with their own eyes, how another musician plays that piece. On stage is on stage—instinct and training and experience take over no matter how informal the setting—but in the Green Room, there is less self-consciousness about being in awe of another player or asking how that was done. In the Green Room, in fact, everyone is so absorbed in the music that the players are reluctant to leave it to go out and play for the crowd.

"Getting a line-up for the Festival Club can be like pulling teeth," says local musician and writer Kelley Edwards, who has managed the Club stage. She describes a memorable scene:

"Finally, Gordie Sampson stands up and announces, 'Okay, I'll go up if Éamonn and Frankie come too. And I'm playing the drums.' So, he heads out to the stage and the others follow. Irishmen Éamonn Coyne with his banjo and ever-present, up-for-anything smile, and Frankie Lane, in velvet and rhinestone pants, a cigar clamped in the side of his mouth, guitar strap half over his shoulder. As they set up they are joined by local players Fred Lavery from Point Aconi on guitar, Mira's Ed Woodsworth who's been playing bass with Ashley MacIsaac's band, and Ashley's sister Lisa MacIsaac on fiddle."

"Gordie wanted to get me and Lisa MacIsaac playing together—it may have been the last night and the last band or something like that," remembers Coyne, though he's not sure that Lane ended up playing in that set. "Fred Lavery was on guitar and that is why I wonder was Frankie involved. But Gordie was indeed on drums and it all went mental from there really. I knew a lot of Cape Breton tunes and stuff from listening to various people over the years so tune combinations were not a huge problem, although there was probably a bit of improv on the go—as was probably also the case for Lisa."

Coyne and Lane had already made their presence known at the festival. They were an unlikely pair for Cape Breton audiences: playing banjo and dobro, neither a common instrument for this land of fiddles and pipes. And neither played by any common folk, but by masters in this case. Dublin-born Éamonn Coyne possesses a Ph.D. in organic chemistry but has made a name for himself playing tunes on the tenor banjo. He has played with many, many artists, regularly touring and performing with American banjo player Alison Brown and with Edinburgh-based Salsa Celtica. And his interest in Old Timey, Americana, and country music led him to record with Béla Fleck and Jerry Douglas in the 1990s, and to play and tour with Frankie Lane.

"This interest brought me to Hughes Pub in Dublin on a Tuesday night where Frankie and Dermy Diamond, a fiddler, used to play and it all stemmed from there. We played at various gigs together over the years before Cape Breton, but have had little time together since 1997 as I now live in Edinburgh and he is still in Dublin."

Frankie Lane makes his mark on dobro, a steel-stringed guitar with a resonator which is played with a glass or steel slide in place of individual finger positions. The instrument may be better known for blues and is the type of guitar pictured on the cover of the famous Dire Straits album *Brothers in Arms* that had that big hit "Money For Nothing." The thing about Frankie Lane, the original front man of the Fleadh Cowboys—who toured supporting Bob Dylan, U2, Emmy Lou Harris and the Pogues during the 1980s—is that he plays Irish tunes on this instrument. His album *Dobro* was the first to feature the instrument in the context of Irish traditional tunes.

Celtic Colours was the duo's second time playing in Cape Breton. "The first time we were over we did Ben Eoin, St. Joseph du Moine and another few places about the same time," says Éamonn. "I had met a lot of Cape Breton musicians while they were visiting Ireland over the years—Tommy Basker, Jerry Holland, Hilda Chiasson, Paul Cranford, Paul MacDonald—and was well keen on visiting. I was on a train journey after a gig in Kerry in Ireland with Brendan Begley and Frankie, and he asked if I knew anything about Cape Breton as his brother lives in Halifax. I told him my bit and he asked if I would be up for going. I contacted Liz Doherty and got Dan MacDonald's details and he invited us to stay and arranged some gigs. We both applied to the Irish Arts

Council for an Aer Lingus travel grant and got it, so off we went. We flew to Halifax and stayed with his brother for a night or two before I caught the bus to Sydney—hellish with a screaming kid for what seemed like nearly all of the eight hours—and Dan picked me up. Next morning Tommy Basker was around to see me and it all kicked off really. Frankie came to Sydney a few days later with his brother's family and we got to playing some music."

This is how these people have come, from different backgrounds and along different paths, to play music together. They share the common knowledge of some tunes—some Jerry Holland tunes no doubt—the playing of fiddler and lighthouse keeper and composer Paul Cranford or guitarist Paul MacDonald, plus the history of music that goes back a few hundred years on this island and at least a few hundred more before it crossed over the ocean. And it becomes the language through which they can communicate. The music has been passed on, passed down, and passed around from generation to generation through playing and sharing what is known and exploring and learning what is unknown. These unfamiliar instruments—whether it's Frankie Lane on dobro or Gordie Sampson on drum kit—mix and match with the better-known elements of Lisa MacIsaac on fiddle and consummate accompanist Fred Lavery on guitar, until something new comes to be, based on what has gone before and staking out new territory of its own. That's the tradition of music on Cape Breton Island. And this tradition continues with the Green Room connections.

"Jennifer Roland, the young fiddler from Alder Point who plays Winston 'Scotty' Fitzgerald's fiddle and who had just released her first album, *Dedication*, and Mary Shannon of the Irish group Bumblebees, are two of the many fiddlers playing in a circle around the piano, accompanied by Doug MacPhee. Cape Breton songwriters Wally MacAulay and Buddy MacDonald—who co-hosts the club stage this year with John Allan Cameron—are beside the stage door, trying to watch both the band on stage and the action happening inside the Green Room, trying to get the best of both worlds. When the band on stage finishes, those musicians pile back into the Green Room, putting their instruments down long enough to grab a beer and compliment each other on a job well done. Then it's back to the circle where, long after the bar has closed, the audience gone home and the lights turned off to make room for the light of day, the music continues."

One morning very early, the sun having been up for a while, the hotel staff were doing their best to clear the rooms in preparation for a big-shot brunch hosted by the former leader of Canada's New Democratic Party. The staff worked at clearing the Celtic Colours debris of the night before off the tables—empty beer cans mostly and makeshift ashtrays—as a few stragglers sat around squeezing out another round or two of tunes. Finally, the staff were ready to vacuum and bring in clean fresh white linen for the morning brunch. But the tunes weren't finished yet. There were still a few cans of beer stashed behind the heavy velvet, floor-length curtains and nearly everyone had at least one can in a pocket or instrument case. No sir, this party isn't over yet. Tell the politician he'll have to wait. The fifteen-minute warning was ignored, or barely noticed, so intense were the tunes.

"Five more minutes, then you have to clear this room."

"Well we ain't got no place to go. And we're gonna keep playing."

The staff came in with the vacuum cleaner and started sucking up near the stomping feet around the piano. There was some resistance to this action. The pipers—'cause there's always a piper or two up until the end of the tunes—were getting itchy. One of the pipers said he couldn't hear the piano over the noise of the vacuum. They started making motions like they were going to go round up their pipes to counter the vacuum and then maybe go parade throughout the hotel, gathering more pipers as they went along to prove their point that sometimes you just gotta let the music be, let it do what it's going to do in the hands of those who hold it dear.

It's not an easy task to argue with such a gathering of pipers, threatening to parade throughout the hotel, pipes a-blasting.

Although it was obviously very late at night for the pipers and assorted other festival stragglers, it was very squarely morning for most of the hotel guests. They had checked in for a night's sleep with things to do the next day. The musicians, on the other hand, had gathered back at the hotel after their show, and everyone followed them back to party—until the wee hours if they could get away with it.

Compromise was reached. The staff found a room suitable for finishing the festivities without a note being blown in the halls. It goes to show the different realities we live in. For the musicians gathered, there was no way the party would end before they were ready. For the hotel staff, well, they had a job to do and they were going to do it.

The Holiday Inn was quite the scene that first year. They had hosted conventions and hockey tournaments, but nothing like this, with a bar in the basement until three in the morning. It took some adjusting!

# It was a perfectly windy, colourful autumn day in Baddeck.

The green was beginning to fade from the vegetation, though the grass and hedges retained enough colour to brilliantly contrast with the invading oranges and deep bright reds of the surrounding trees. The day would prove itself . . . .

My first assignment as a volunteer Celtic Colours driver for this year was to take Scottish Gaelic singers Ishbel MacAskill and Margaret Bennett for an afternoon drive down the Cabot Trail to see the autumn leaves. We made it as far as Wreck Cove, looking for *Cape Breton's Magazine* publisher Ron Caplan, with whom Margaret had corresponded quite extensively on a project in the past. She was thrilled at the prospect of meeting him face to face. In addition to being a beautifully-voiced Gaelic singer, Margaret is a much respected scholar, folklorist and writer who has had books published about Scottish emigration to Canada and Scottish customs. Margaret has returned to the festival again and again, to sing and to conduct workshops in Gaelic song and Scottish traditions.

Tom Knapp described Margaret as spinning stories "with an easy manner, painting pictures in the air, and engrossing the audience in timeless tales of their shared Gaelic heritage. Her gleaming eyes reflected the constant smile on her face, all under rich, silvery hair. After first relating the stories—often also recalling the way in which she herself first heard them—Bennett then sang the songs unaccompanied, in a pure, sweet Gaelic. She sometimes provided partial translations or taught the audience a line of the chorus, and on those occasions the room filled with the sound of rough, enthusiastic voices. The result was beautiful, spellbinding."

We didn't meet up with Caplan that day—she found him later

at a workshop at Cape Breton University—but we had a lovely afternoon of sightseeing. As we drove, we listened to *The Second Wave*—a compilation of some of the artists who would be performing at Celtic Colours that year—and discussed the various artists represented and their music. When the Gaelic milling song "Cruinneag Na Buaile" came on, somewhere along the North Shore, Margaret and Ishbel praised the group of Cape Breton singers— recorded live off the floor at Christmas Island during Féis an Eilein—that "they know all 150 verses and their accents sound just like they're from Uist" or something to that effect, and their conversation switched seamlessly into Gaelic. I hardly noticed the transition or the difference, although I realized that I could no longer understand what they were saying in the back seat.

A few days later I found myself on the road to Glendale. Laura Risk, in town to play with the John Whelan Band, wanted to see the Alex Francis MacKay tribute called "There's Gaelic in the Fiddle." Our conversation got me thinking about the phrase "living tradition." Risk, a fiddler from San Francisco, was thrilled at the chance to see MacKay play. "He's still *alive?*" she asked in mild disbelief. We discussed the Gaelic in the fiddle without really meaning to. I was initially a little amused by the fact that this Californian was a student of Cape Breton fiddle music. Indeed, she knew much more about it than I did. We talked about immigration and migration, oral tradition versus book learning, collections of tunes before and after the 1840s and '50s, and finally the culture and history of Cape Breton Island. We tried to identify some of the things that have influenced Cape Breton's traditional music, tracing the tunes to their Scottish roots, in this case. We got to the hall a few minutes later and there was a crowd gathered outside. Coincidently, they were from California and recognized Risk from sessions around the Bay area—San Francisco Bay, not Glace Bay. They were surprised to run into each other like that, but like I told them, this is what happens on Cape Breton Island. It's a small world, and all that. This crowd was standing outside the door in the mist, without tickets for the show, and were happy enough to be where they were as the music traveled out the door, occasionally drowned out by transport trucks speeding by on Trans-Canada Highway's Route 105.

Guitarist Paul MacDonald did a lovely job hosting that show. With story after story, MacDonald brought to life people and players of the time while introducing those taking part in the tribute, contemporary players like Dave MacIsaac and Dougie MacDonald and Jeff MacDonald and Mary Jane Lamond and Mairi MacInnes and Fred Morrison. During intermission I saw for myself how some of these traditions are passed along—out in the parking lot, gathered around the trunk of a car, chased with a can of pop—and I thought of my naiveté only the year before when I was surprised to find out that "Celtic" musicians sometimes behaved like "rock stars."

When the Celtic Colours Festival headquarters moved to Baddeck, festival staff practically took over the Inverary Inn, with offices in one end of the MacAulay Centre, the Festival Club stage and the Green Room at the other end of the building. During the day, Iain Anderson, a well-known BBC radio personality, recorded performances produced by Wendy Bergfeldt, host of CBC radio's afternoon program *Mainstreet*. An audience was invited in and performers were interviewed on stage.

At night, the Festival Club came alive in that same room. With a scheduled closing time determined by the liquor laws of Nova Scotia—a very strict closing time—the staff had no choice but to cut off sales according to the clock. If you were wise enough, however, to buy before last call, you were welcome to stay and finish your drinks past closing time. And once you got the hang of it, you were more inclined to stock up a bit because, as we were all about to learn, music isn't restricted by the clock and would often go on beyond the reasonable. It wasn't unusual for the sun to be peeking through the windows before the session broke up and the stragglers made their way to breakfast.

When the Festival Club was at the Holiday Inn, sometimes

1. Mike Elliott
2. Sierra Noble
3. Bruce Guthro
4. Pierre Schryer
5. Lisa MacIsaac
6. Daniel Lapp
7. Harald Haugaard
8. Natalie Haas
9. Liz Doherty
10. Patricia Chafe
11. Chris Stout
12. Karan Casey
13. Tim Edey &
    Catriona McKay

1. Angus Grant
2. Bobby Roper
3. Maybelle Chisholm MacQueen
4. Shane Cook
5. Phil "Flipper" Frumignac
6. Liam Ó Maonlaí
7. Allie Bennett
8. Rachel Davis
9. Douglas Cameron
10. Kenneth MacKenzie
11. Peter Gillis
12. (l to r) Jerry Holland, John Doyle, Carl MacKenzie, Andrea Beaton, John Donald Cameron, Courtney Granger, Kinnon Beaton, Tommy Sands, John Joe Kelly.

13. Pascal Miousse
14. Gern f.
15. Stewart MacNeil
16. Margaret Bennett
17. David Francey
18. Gay McKeon
19. Joella Foulds &
    Ron Hynes
20. Fred Lavery
21. Dwayne Côté
22. Kyle MacNeil
23. (l to r) Colin Carrigan,
    Jim Payne, Graham Wells,
    Gerry Strong and
    Fergus O'Byrne

1. Ellen MacPhee
2. John Ferguson
3. Rosie MacKenzie
4. Max MacDonald
5. Ronald Bourgeois
6. Manus McGuire
7. Old Man Luedecke
8. Paul Brock
9. Doug MacPhee
10. Bruce MacGregor
11. Winnie Chafe
12. Ryan J. MacNeil
13. (l to r) Anna Massie,
    Allan Henderson,
    Jenna Reid,
    Bruce MacGregor,
    Iain MacFarlane

14. Gordie Sampson
15. Jenna Reid
16. Joe Peter MacLean
17. Allan Henderson
18. Moya Brennan
19. Terry Kelly
20. Stephen Muise
21. Jennifer Roland
22. Anna Massie
23. Buddy MacDonald &
    John Allan Cameron
24. Nigel Davey
25. Pascal Gemme and
    Alexandre de
    Grosbois-Garand

1. Ashley MacIsaac
2. Dave MacIsaac
3. Troy MacGillivray
4. Fiona MacGillivray
5. Karine Polwart
6. Phil Cunningham
7. Jimmy Breaux
8. Bruce Molsky
9. Dougie MacLean
10. Sheila Kay Adams
11. Michael Black
12. Colin Grant

13. Emily Smith
14. Rod C. MacNeil
15. Mairéad Ní Mhaonaigh
16. Carlos Núñez
17. Hilda Chiasson-
    Cormier
18. Joe Newberry
19. Rita MacNeil
20. Dawn Beaton
21. Judique Community
    Centre
22. Nic Gareiss

1. Lewis MacKinnon
2. Tommy Sands
3. Marion Dewar
4. John MacLean
5. John Donald Cameron
6. Ryan MacDonald
7. Aonghas Grant
8. Tim Edey & Bill Elliott
9. David Papazian
10. Lucy MacNeil
11. Victor Tomiczek, Dave Mahalik, Donnie Calabrese

12. Nuala Kennedy
13. John C. (Jack) O'Donnell
    & The Men of the Deeps
14. Archie Fisher
15. Michael Doucet
16. Niamh Ní Charra
17. Steven MacDougall
18. Ian MacDougall
19. Sylvie Doucet
20. Alasdair Fraser
21. Jerry Holland,
    Dave MacIsaac,
    Theresa MacLellan,
    Donald MacLellan

1. Community Volunteers serving up a meal
2. Paul Cranford
3. Allie Mombourquette
4. Haley MacPhee
5. Wally MacAulay & Doug Johnson
6. Scott Macmillan
7. Otis Tomas
8. Andrea Beaton
9. J.P. Cormier & Bill Elliott

10. Tim O'Brien
11. Kathryn Tickell
12. Matt Minglewood
13. Sharon Shannon
14. Chelle Smith, Kelley Edwards,
    & Amy Sampson having a laugh
    backstage at the Festival Club
15. Margie Beaton
16. Catriona McKay leading a harp
    workshop at the Gaelic College
17. Donnie Campbell
18. Brenda Stubbert &
    Paul MacDonald

1. Deanie Cox
2. Howie MacDonald
3. Raylene Rankin
4. Marcel Nazabal
5. Joey Beaton
6. Kris Drever &
   Dougie MacLean
7. Mary Jane Lamond
8. Paddy Moloney
9. Seán McKeon
10. Wendy MacIsaac,
    Mairi Rankin,
    Natalie MacMaster

the staff there just didn't know what to make of it all. Security at the hotel didn't even try to understand that the music must go on, that what Celtic Colours had gathered here were musicians separated at birth, reunited for the first time, and that they were going to sit down and play together until they got reacquainted. At the Inverary Inn, the staff didn't even ask, they just let it go, seeming to understand that the music's just gotta happen, past liquor hours, past rides home, past no smokes. Well, maybe not past no smokes, but in a room full of people who want nothing but a session, things have a way of taking care of themselves.

When it gets right down to it the Festival Club night ceases to be night. But it's not morning either. The morning doesn't come around till it's time for bed.

The Festival Club depends on a moment in time—that moment when the magic happens. It's an unpredictable thing, this magic. It depends on who's who, where they are and when. Each moment only ever happens once. But there are lots of them. You could see it had happened in Liz Doherty's face, when she came off the stage after twenty minutes onstage with Altan. Altan is a group that comes from her home area and, as it turned out, she had always wanted to play with them. The next time the magic struck, it was different, an unusual combination of performers, perhaps performers gathered together from half a dozen countries.

It's a popular story that Beòlach came to be during an impromptu session at the Celtic Colours Festival Club late one night in Baddeck. "It started as a whim and became a life-changing decision," wrote Tom Knapp. "Wendy MacIsaac, already an established Cape Breton fiddler, joined an informal pick-up band on the stage of the Festival Club at the 1999 Celtic Colours Festival. Such bands are formed and disbanded every day during the weeklong festival, but this one was different. The members clicked and decided to make it an ongoing effort. 'It was a slow night,' MacIsaac recalls. 'A group of us got up and played a bunch of tunes. That's how it started.'"

And later Kaitlin Hahn, a fiddler from Wisconsin, wrote, "To me Beòlach is probably the most creative Celtic band out there today, in terms of how they arrange their tunes. I never get bored when I listen to them. Their shows include a wonderful mix of traditional and modern, fast and slow, and because there are five people in the band, different instrumental arrangements. The variety is amazing. As I was watching them, I kept thinking, 'Wow! I can't really pick a favourite set, because they're all really good,' but then, at the very end of the show, they did a number where Mairi Rankin, Mac Morin and Wendy MacIsaac all got up and danced. That was definitely my favourite. It, too, ended in a standing ovation."

One of the "true hearts" of the festival, wrote Mike Morrison in his article "Invasion of the Sleepless Funnytalkers," "revealed itself in the form of a couple of sleepless nights. Over the course of these nights, nights that went far into the morning, what really seemed to represent this festival for anyone who was there, was a sort of after-hours festival and a chance to meet some great folks and hear some amazing music unbound by the ominous steel fist of the stage manager. This was music as a common language, used by people from across the island, the country and the ocean with no need for practice or even many spoken words to communicate. I don't know if everyone who came wanted to make sure they got their money's worth for their plane tickets or what, but there was no way the fun was going to shut down with the show. Music at the Festival Club, a sort of home base at Baddeck's Inverary Inn, went on until four a.m., and impromptu jams stretched well into the light of morning. One older fellow commented, 'I must be an old fool. I should be home in my bed but I just ordered a gin.' I guess we must have been a bunch of fools, old and young. Another conversation I heard went something like this: Question: 'Do you drink rum?' Answer: 'I *will* drink rum.'"

Like on the first night. The staged entertainment had ended, but we were welcome to hang around and finish our drinks. Paul MacDonald had lost his guitar but Liz had another fiddler with her and Lauchie had more drink stashed in his car and the staff quietly cleaned up behind us. Eventually, Paul got another guitar and the night continued . . . .

And so it went, night after night, no two quite the same. By 4 a.m., you knew what was going on. The stage shuts down or it doesn't, and the bar is open here or across the way at the Lakeside Café. And the music will continue. This would become Fred Lavery's domain, night after night, encouraging the session along with his guitar, prompting another tune out of Liz Doherty and Clare McLaughlin, pushing, ever so slightly, for Tony McManus to treat us one more time, and then leading the charge to breakfast. Breakfast could be an experience in itself, both for those tourists fresh from a night's sleep, ready for a leisurely day of sightseeing into their golden years on one of the many buses parked outside, and for we wild-eyed and weary festival-goers, getting a bite before bed as the sun comes up to threaten our souls.

I missed Alasdair Fraser and Liz Doherty with Altan. I wasn't there the night Alasdair and Tony McManus played together, or closing night when Boyd MacNeil got up with his brothers and sister. But even if you were there every night you couldn't see everything. The real joy was just being there, amid the energy and experience, inside outside upside down, from the bar to the Green Room behind the stage and across to the café. Every single performance was unique, a once-in-a-lifetime happening. Like sitting around the tables at the Festival Club long past closing time and Tony McManus is picking at a tune. Looks of pure joy are exchanged across the table and around the room as he coaxes a recognizable melody out of the air. I sat with Angelo Spinazzola in the back one night and we marveled at the beauty of it all, the musical highlights, the mishmash of odd pairings, unusual performance choices and the sheer stamina of folks like Bumblebees sharing their musical *craic* until night turns to day.

One year, Kelley Edwards wrote: "The Festival Club venue was the MacAulay Centre at the Inverary Inn. The ceilings were high and the room spacious, making the atmosphere most agreeable. The backstage area was not as large as the previous year's, and in this case, that wasn't a bad thing. There were still small sessions happening in the Green Room, but the enchantment took place, believe it or not, on the stage.

"Because last year's session room was so large, hardly anyone, except for the paying public, sat in the audience. This year, performers raced out front to get a seat and encourage their peers. Naturally all the music was topnotch, but several performances stand out as never-to-be-captured-again moments in musical history.

"The earliest happening was with Altan, the band from Ireland, whose heat and intensity earned them a previously unheard-of two standing ovations from the crowd. Another moment that stands out was so sweet it almost left an ache when it was over. Guitarist Tony McManus and fiddler Alasdair Fraser sat down for a set . . . . As the last strains of their music died away, a unanimous sigh could be felt through the audience. Throughout the entire festival, many people played instruments, but this was the first time I had ever heard them speak to me as another language. This was pure communication, first between two artists, and then to a sea of waiting hearts."

Here are three takes on a single event. Kelley Edwards: "In a totally last-minute and spontaneous venture, our own Gordie Sampson went one-on-one with John Whelan, guitar and accordion, respectively, and proceeded to set fire to the room. Sampson played notes that I'm sure were unheard of until that moment, much to the delight of Whelan who, like the mischievous kid on the playground, almost dared him on. In fact, both men went gleefully note to note, head to head and eye to eye for forty-five minutes straight. It was pure euphoria as they grinned and laughed out loud. At the end the stage was soaked with sweat and whatever beverages were upset by stomping feet."

Fred Lavery: "Gordie Sampson and Clare McLaughlin (Deaf Shepherd) had just done a smokin' set of tunes together that had everyone shakin' their heads. As they were leaving the stage John Whelan, virtuoso accordion player, asked Gordie to go up and play with him. They proceeded to tear the place apart. You could almost see the total mental and musical lock between them. You could certainly hear it!! I don't think I've ever seen anything so incredibly powerful that was totally spontaneous from two inspired performers who had never played together before."

Buddy MacDonald: "Musically, the moment that really stands out in my memory is the year the Festival Club was in Baddeck and John Whelan the box player and our own Gordie Sampson teamed up for an impromptu session of monster proportions. They played over half an hour of flawless tunes, throwing grins and chords across the stage like a well-rehearsed act, although at this point they had never even met each other and had no idea that the other even existed musically. At the end of the set they embraced to a standing ovation from an audience that had just been witness to another magical moment in the history of Celtic Colours. I was at the edge of the stage as they came off and John turned to me and with a look of awe on his face said, 'Now what planet is that young guitar player from?' Sort of summed it all up."

Kelley Edwards continued: "There were other terrific moments, such as Eleanor Shanley's clear and haunting voice as she sang about the Magdalene Laundry. There was Corrina Hewat and David Milligan's funky jazz Celtic duo of harp and piano. And of course there is never a shortage of magic in the tunes when the Bumblebees are around, due not only to their style of playing, but to their infectious energy and fun.

"A few nights during the Festival Club, the stage had to be shut down at 4 a.m., but not the tunes. Everyone was encouraged to make a short walk across the parking lot to the Lakeside Café, and there amidst the checkered tablecloths, the windows overlooking the moored sailboats, the sessions went on. This was pegged by Stephen MacDonald as 'Festival Club unplugged.' Who will forget Paul Cranford, Tommy Basker, Mary Shannon and Clare McLaughlin playing and smiling as they shared one tune after another?

"On the very last night (or should I say morning) of the Festival, as the sun was waking up, and a thin mist still slept upon the water, Pierre Schryer stood up alone and played unaccompanied, a slow and beautiful air—his lament, he said, for leaving Cape Breton."

The first load of troops got back to headquarters in record time Friday night after taking in the "Celtic Connections" show at the Savoy Theatre. They were ready for the mission—got to bed just after the sun came up and were out of bed by noon. Not even a little bit tired.

We're starting to get the hang of this, what do you mean it's almost over?

It's true. Another festival is coming to a close. Just three more concerts left. A lot of ground has been covered in just a little over a week. We introduced some new artists to a lot of people, presented some favourites from years gone by, and showed a lot about the connections that make this world of music tick.

So there's one more day left. While the crews are putting the finishing touches on the Baddeck Arena Saturday afternoon for the "World's Biggest Square Dance," the pipers will gather on the grounds of the Gaelic College for the "Pipers' Ceildih" and the "Next Generation" of talent will be featured at Strathspey Place in Mabou. And that will be it. Another Celtic Colours International Festival will be history.

But first: "The World's Biggest Square Dance"—the last show of the festival from its introduction in 1998 until 2003. According to Robin Bullock of the John Whelan Band, the billing is possibly a misnomer. Robin told me about a festival in the States that had performers on three stages, simultaneously playing a jig for the Guinness Book of World Records. They had a huge crowd, all "doing a jig" at the same time. I didn't bother explaining the difference between "doing a jig" and a Cape Breton square dance. He'd see for himself as the night progressed.

One year when we held the dance at the Victoria Highland Civic Centre in Baddeck, the sign outside—probably the same one they use for bingo—read "Colossal Square Dance." An army of enthusiastic volunteers had treated that local hockey rink to curtains and banners and spinnakers hanging from the rafters.

"This is what it's all about," said John Whelan—the rink transformed into a cozy, comfy atmosphere. He actually told me he likes this kind of gig much more than any of the "glitzy" ones he sometimes plays, so much better than Carnegie Hall, for instance, which is "so stuffy." It harkens back to an older time, he recalled, to barn dances and summers in Ireland as a teenager.

Prompter Burton MacIntyre did a great job keeping some order among the chaos. With a lighted platform in front of the stage and two floor instructors, he led hundreds of dancers through the sets and various styles of Cape Breton square dancing—the Mabou style and the Sydney style on the go in the same set with music by some of the island's best dance players, like Buddy MacMaster on his birthday, Kinnon and Betty Lou Beaton, Carl MacKenzie, Glenn Graham and Rodney MacDonald, Doug MacPhee, Paul K. MacNeil and Jamie MacInnis. Dave MacIsaac and Tracey Dares were joined by Kate Dunlay, David Greenberg, Richard Wood and Stuart Cameron. Top that!

With John Allan Cameron hosting, the audience enjoyed performances by Gordie Sampson and Ed Woodsworth with a few songs from Sampson's new album *Stones*, Slainte Mhath, John Whelan Band and Pierre Schryer.

Whelan was in his element, marveling at the opportunity to meet people—he even spent some time at the door taking tickets—and to learn some tunes from fellow musicians. As the crowd came through the door, he was busy with the stamp that marks who's paid.

"Is he always like this?" someone asked bassist Tom Wetmore.

"John really loves people," he replied.

Preparations for a "World's Biggest Square Dance" in Baddeck mean a team of professionals and volunteers converts an arena into a dance hall. A school class from Baddeck helps set up the chairs and tables which are transported from Cape Breton University's Canada Games Complex and from Bayplex in Glace Bay. Tommy MacKinnon and his crew from Centre 200 work on setting up the stage. Volunteers provide everything from food for the crews and artists to decorating the arena, taking tickets, and selling merchandise.

"We get huge support from Sam Morrison at the arena, support from the Bell Museum, and Sheldon MacDonald of Baddeck Building Supplies," says Bill Appleby who spent all day at the site. Bill is coordinating production of the show as well as stage managing.

"We started dropping things off Wednesday. Today we started building the stage and lighting trusses, and we had a rigger on site to set up the spinnakers."

The colourful spinnakers—the large triangular sail set at the front of racing yachts—are donated by the yachting community through Micky Woodford to help transform the arena, usually used for skating, hockey and the occasional bingo game, into a space more suitable for a musical celebration. Work will continue until showtime.

"Tomorrow we continue preparing the arena and decorating. And then it really gets nuts Saturday morning. The rest of the sound and lighting equipment is loaded in and set up. All morning and into the early afternoon we finish setting up the lights and sound, aiming spotlights, getting the sound equalized. Then the sound-checks start. The tables and chairs get set up. And the doors open at eight o'clock."

When the show is over at one o'clock in the morning, the crew from CorDon Sound and the staging crew from Centre 200 start tearing down immediately. The gear will be loaded into trucks that night.

According to Bill it could take until four a.m. On Sunday, crews will come in to take down everything else—the tables and chairs and spinnakers and decorations. Five days of work for one night of fun. Is it worth it? You betcha!

Another late night at the Festival Club I overheard Altan's manager talking about doing away with the stage and the lights and the sound system and stripping down to a more traditional Irish Pub session where musicians just sit around at a table with their instruments and play. He kind of got his wish when the sessions started up again over at the Lakeside Café, practically impromptu but, I'm sure, craftily planned by Festival Club manager Stephen MacDonald as a solution for getting the boot from the main room on account of an early morning function.

By day, the Lakeside Café is a buttoned-down, slightly upscale café with windows overlooking the waters of Baddeck Bay. On this very early morning, everyone who was still game tramped over to the café with instruments and last drinks in tow. With the sun coming up, tunes were exchanged—a couple of Bumblebees, Tommy Basker, Paul Cranford, Pierre Schryer—just sitting around playing tunes. It turned out to be a great place for late-night chats or to really have a conversation with someone. The music really took over centre stage—and without amplification. I talked about art and drawing, music and writing and intoxicants, late one night with Conrad Ivitsky, bass player with Shooglenifty, at Celtic Colours accompanying Shetland fiddler Catriona Macdonald. Another night it was all about the production of music festivals with Carsten Panduro of Denmark's long-running Tønder Festival. This space wasn't advertised as Open For Business, but if you knew about it, you belonged there.

By now, Dear Reader, you must be asking yourself: How can a busy guy like me take time off from work to spend a week driving around the island? Actually, I can't afford not to. After all, I'm the managing editor of Cape Breton's arts-and-entertainment magazine. And what better way to get an overview of the festival? I can direct and manage the magazine's coverage on the run. I love the opportunity to spread word among performers, especially those first-timers from away, that we exist and will possibly be featuring them in upcoming issues. And it's a fine way to meet new, interesting people.

So, with my little green hospital-like wristband to open doors, and my daily instructions regarding who to take where, and when, I'm meeting people like Vida Elisson from Reykjavik, Iceland, who has already become a fixture at the festival; Gaelic singer and folklorist Margaret Bennett; and American fiddler Laura Risk whose enthusiasm for Cape Breton fiddle music overflowed into a nearly academic discussion as we drove toward Glendale.

And the driving was nice, in brand new vehicles rented from Budget Rent-a-Car. One afternoon was spent along the Cabot Trail just to show off the Fall colours to visitors. Other times the drive was from Baddeck to Louisbourg or Glace Bay and back. The weather and scenery combined with my continuing discovery of the back story of settlement on this island, stimulated by my passengers' observations. "This is just like America," someone from the John Whelan Band noticed on the way back to Sydney from Glace Bay's Savoy Theatre, as we hit Welton Street at night, with its fast food and car dealerships. Sometimes it's just the karma, like on a Tim Horton's run with Corrina Hewat in Glace Bay, and Captain Kirk suddenly cuts through the radio static singing "Lucy in the Sky with Diamonds." Or it's just the collision of conversation, as Eleanor Shanley, John McLoughlin and John's wife debrief the events of the day. It can be as simple as just catching up with an old friend like Laoise Kelly on the long road from Louisbourg to Baddeck in the dark.

Another year, and again another Festival Club is hopping, night after night, hosted by North Shore singer/songwriter Buddy MacDonald. Only four nights into one year's festival, crowds have already been treated to unusual combinations of players. One night, Mad Pudding got things off on the right foot—and the left one too—with a rollicking set of highly danceable tunes.

Saturday night saw more and more artists showing up, blessed by Kelley the Ceilidh Faerie who presided over the room outfitted in wand and tiara, sprinkling her magic dust all around. As well as encouraging silly costumes, and general good-natured shenanigans, she made sure the punch bowl was full and even brought in her own home baking for special treats.

Goosebumps as John Allan Cameron joined the 8 Wing Trenton Pipe Band for "Chi Mi na Mor Bheanna." The Pipe Band was travelling in a convoy of festival vehicles after their bus's engine caught fire.

That same night Slainte Mhath's Ryan and Boyd MacNeil took the stage by storm with Matt Foulds on percussion and Paul MacDonald on guitar. Soon Joannie Madden of Cherish the Ladies was whistling along with them. A square set broke out and the night was flying, late as it was.

Sunday night's Festival Club was treated to the much-awaited Cherish the Ladies and Paddy Keenan and Sean Tyrrell. Tunes were let out of the box when accordionist Joe Derrane and guitarist Paul MacDonald took over the stage.

Staff picks for Monday evening were the incredible performances by Alasdair Codona—an inspiring a cappella selection of Gaelic song—and much later an intense performance by Sean Tyrrell on mandocello. All that can be said of Jes Kroman's fiddle set with accompaniment artfully provided by John Allan Cameron is "Jes! Jes! Jes!" Tuesday morning was brought in by a rousing version of "You Are My Sunshine" led by Kelley Edwards and Mairi MacInnes—and many Gaels joined the ensuing conga line.

In the daylight, the Festival Club served as a radio station for BBC Radio Scotland, who taped *The Iain Anderson Show* and *A Cape Breton Christmas Card* special. And all that week, Wendy Bergfeldt, host of CBC Radio One's *Mainstreet*, made recordings and broadcast live from the Festival Club.

Wednesday saw another late night, with tunes till the wee hours. Jennifer and Hazel Wrigley blew the lid off the place with a set that defied description but inspired a standing ovation. Bachue followed and after performing as a duo, collaborated with the sisters from Orkney.

Thursday night was so full of music, it is hard to know where to begin. Gibb Todd, our visiting Festival Club co-host from Celtic

Connections, sang a few lovely songs before Dougie MacLean took the stage and blessed us with two beautiful original songs including "Ready for the Storm," which seemed more than appropriate given the weather of the day.

Llan de Cubel had a great set, an exotic treat during an evening that has since been dubbed "Cape Breton night." Jennifer Roland and a kickass band had something to do with that for sure; she captured the hearts of visitors who had never had the pleasure. Mary Jane Lamond dazed and amazed the appreciative audience with an impromptu collection of former band members, closing with an incredible arrangement of "Sleepy Maggie." "The hot chicks and their house boys" was how host Gibb Todd presented Mairi Rankin, Mac Morin, Lisa MacIsaac, Ed Woodsworth, Paddy Gillis and Matt Foulds. It was music made for dancing as Joella got a square set going with Alasdair Fraser.

Dan Crary's quote of the night was: "I think you people may be enjoying yourselves too much."

Tom Knapp wrote: "It's possible to enjoy the music and splendour of Celtic Colours without attending a single concert . . . . There's no predicting what might happen when the spotlight hits the Festival Club stage. Some musicians give encore performances from their usual set list. Others take the opportunity to explore, experimenting with styles and joining forces with other musicians to form incredible pickup bands. Sometimes, silliness abounds.

"Try to find someone who heard Brian McNeill's 'Mason's Apron' set, a fiddle medley not available on any McNeill CD, that explored a lot of possibilities up to and including 'The Hall of the Mountain King.' See who was there when Bruce MacGregor, a fiddler with Blazin' Fiddles and Cliar, stripped off his pants to inspire musicians on stage to new heights.

"Members of the Irish band Danú gathered onstage with several Cape Breton musicians for an energetic improv set. Kimberley Fraser, a young Cape Breton fiddler, joined forces with Danish duo Haugaard & Høirup for a grand blast of tunes—despite little time to rehearse. And who can forget young fiddler Ian MacDougall's 40-plus-minute set, a continuous blast of energetic tunes that started with Buddy MacDonald and Mac Morin accompanying him on guitar and piano, and ended with more than a dozen musicians packed on stage for the jam."

From Tony McManus's online diary:

"Back at the Festival Club Phil Cunningham is winning friends and influencing people. Ever in search of hilarity, Phil has decided that it would be a wheeze if two or more random Scottish musicians were to walk on front and centre, take the applause meant for whoever happens to be on stage and then walk off. Sadly there are lots of volunteers, including myself. Before long 'applause theft' is the new craze in Cape Breton.

"The festival even provides for those demented souls who can't quite bring themselves to go to bed after the club shuts down at 3:30 a.m. There is the Tune Shack—basically a hut with a piano, some chairs and lots of punters playing till the sun comes up.

"At a festival like this there's usually one band or one musician that has everyone saying 'did you hear . . . ?' At Celtic Colours 2001 Daniel Lapp was that man! Mr. Lapp is from Vancouver and plays a mean fiddle, at this festival alongside the equally mean fiddle of Donegal's own Liz Doherty. At the festival club, though, it wasn't just the fiddling that had tongues wagging, not to mention ears flapping. Towards the end of their already blistering set Daniel put down the fiddle and picked up the trumpet! 'What the hell is he going to do with that?' I thought to myself, as did a few hundred others.

"Daniel proceeded to play fiddle tunes in a way I'd not have thought possible."

# Then there was the headline in *The Daily News*: "Rave out, Icon in at Celtic Colours fest"

Sandy MacDonald wrote in "Behind the Beat":

And, by the way, there are disagreements. One year, festival organizers couldn't shake hands over a contract. Though the international Celtic-music festival was the brainchild of Rave's Max MacDonald and Joella Foulds, Icon Communications was now handling the nuts and bolts of the festival.

What happened to take the event out of the hands of the people who conceived and operated it for four years?

"Quite frankly, we're mystified," said MacDonald.

But Celtic Colours chairman Sam MacPhee wasn't: "It was a business decision. The previous management didn't agree with our offer . . . and elected not to come on board."

The roots of the split go back to the festival's inception. Rave had conceived the idea of an autumn Celtic festival, inspired by Cape Breton's growing international reputation for musicianship, natural beauty and hospitality.

With a business plan in place, Rave approached the province in 1997 for funding through the Celebration of Music program, a two-year provincial tourism initiative.

"Everyone agreed Celtic Colours was a wonderful idea that would benefit tourism," said MacDonald. "However, the Department of Economic Development said it could not get involved with a private company."

So MacDonald and Foulds formed the Celtic Colours Festival Society, and registered the copyrights of the festival name and logo under the non-profit society. In exchange for those copyrights, Rave signed a five-year management agreement with the newly minted board of directors.

Celtic Colours was then able to access provincial funding and launched the first event with a $600,000 budget.

The year before, Celtic Colours hired an executive director to take some of the load off the eleven-member board.

"We were asked to put together a quote for our services, which was twenty percent less than what we were paid last year," explains MacDonald. "We felt it was fair because certain of our responsibilities would be done by the executive director."

In March, Rave was informed its quote was "totally unacceptable," said MacDonald, and the board had already determined a budget figure to run the event.

"That (figure) was impossible for us; we'd have lost money. We had until the close of business that day to either accept or reject. There would be no negotiation."

Rave reluctantly opted out of the festival.

Though MacPhee would not discuss the terms of the contract in question, he said the dispute was over money.

"Absolutely, it was dollars. They had the opportunity to say yes or no."

According to MacPhee, when Rave opted not to renew its management arrangement, "we then turned a different direction."

The board contracted Icon, which had done marketing for the festival in previous years, to handle the booking, scheduling and marketing of the 2000 Celtic Colours Festival.

The loss of the festival was a blow to Rave.

"The Celtic Colours contract was a substantial part of our business, and the short term effects were extremely painful," says MacDonald. "But it's been more painful emotionally for us. We worked heart and soul for five years to develop a positive story for Cape Breton, and we were thrown out on the street. It makes you wonder why you do what you do."

But the Celtic Colours International Festival proved more powerful than any contention. It survived.

The festival moved to the Gaelic College in 2000. I wouldn't see the set-up on that campus until 2001. Icon Communications was hired to produce the festival, over Rave Entertainment. I wasn't asked to be part of the team that year.

Then Rave was re-hired in 2001, and I was back on the job. Joella and Max were back as well.

They were back, and fired up with new ideas, such as having annual Artists in Residence—people who would be at Celtic Colours for the entire nine days. The Artists in Residence would be there, not just for two or three performances, but to make a contribution almost every day of the festival. As Joella Foulds said: "Artists in Residence play a role that goes beyond performing to provide an educational and developmental dimension to the Festival." They would meet with groups face to face, give talks and workshops, teach their instrument or their particular interest in Celtic history and lore.

This was a chance for the festival to offer something deeper, more personal—and the Artists in Residence have proved to be a tremendous success.

The first two Artists in Residence were Cape Breton's Mary Jane Lamond, who brought a lifetime of devotion to Gaelic song and a commitment to keeping it alive in today's world, and Scottish guitar genius Tony McManus.

Gaelic language has always been an integral part of the festival, as it is an obviously important aspect of the culture, as well as having its own artistic and entertainment value. "Having Mary Jane as an Artist in Residence had a major impact on the planning of the Festival," says Joella. "Her involvement made us look very carefully at every Gaelic aspect of the programming."

Tony McManus remembered his Celtic Colours years with pure joy: "I taught a two-hour master class which was great fun, but as Artist in Residence I taught a bunch of guitarists for a few days of instruction, with a view to a public performance at the end of the course.

"Six students, four of whom came up from the US.... One difficulty in this type of situation is that the students are all at very different levels and each deserves the same attention. One of the group I know well. Michael Reschetnik from Boulder, Colorado, has been at two camps I've taught at in California and also came to Glasgow for the classes I taught at Celtic Connections.

"Immediately, a young kid from Whycocomagh, Cape Breton, catches my ear. Ian Hayes is a very gifted 17-year-old guitarist—not remotely traditional, his playing is infused with blues licks I could never pull off. This will be fun.

"Over the course of things we cover a bunch of different tunings and ideas and picking techniques and *tunes*! 'Tullochgorum' arranged for seven guitars has to be heard. Archie Fisher heard us play together and compared the sound to a huge hammered dulcimer. Fine by me. Michael has a beautiful arrangement of a Neil Gow lament which we played as a duet in Glasgow—sounds even better with more guitars."

Tony's second day of workshops ended just in time for him to get ready for his duties as emcee of "Music for the Angels." "That concert was in a beautiful old white wooden church in North River," Tony recalled. "A very special venue for me as it was my friends Nicole and Angelo who got the place into shape for concerts. One of the great things about this festival is the special places the musicians get to play in. Reminds me of Shetland. The church was lit by candlelight and looked spectacular."

Again and again, the artists and the audience remarked on the rare settings for Celtic Colours performances. Looking back, Scottish folklorist Margaret Bennett, another Artist in Residence, wrote: "The fire hall at Christmas Island may not sound like a venue for music and songs—but the whole place reverberates, especially when the milling table stretches down the middle and the songs start. Some of the participants are into their seventies and eighties, and it's a privilege to sit among them. One after another, they sing songs that have weathered many a Cape Breton winter. I doubt if last year's Artist in Residence, Jeff MacDonald, would disagree with me, that it would be hard to find a finer example of handing on tradition. He himself is a great testimony to a younger generation who understands the value of it—not only does Jeff speak Gaelic, he has a really good voice and repertoire of songs, but also stories, *sgeulachdan*, which he tells in the style of the *seanchaidh*."

One year, Margaret was paired as Artist in Residence with Cape Breton's fiddler Jerry Holland.

Margaret Bennett embodies a lot of what this festival is all about. She grew up surrounded by the music, in a house where music was played all the time by the grown-ups around her. That was where the party was; where there was music.

Margaret said: "I share with the older generation a belief that real wealth lies within the inherited cultural wealth—music, song, dance, poetry, language and faith that nurtured our people for centuries. Since we are heirs to this enviable heritage I believe we have a responsibility to care for it and pass it on."

That was the sixth Celtic Colours International Festival. It opened with a bang at Centre 200 in Sydney when Margaret and Jerry got things underway in fine style with a lovely Gaelic song and a blast of fiddle tunes.

After them, J.P. Cormier and Hilda Chiasson-Cormier kept the energy up as J.P. went through an awesome display of mastery over stringed instruments.

Fraya Thomsen and Fiona Hunter, students at the Royal Scottish Academy in Glasgow, Scotland, played harp and sang in the main concourse during intermission. They weren't really hired as performers, but were studying and playing around, and Fraya and Fiona became the most photographed people of the festival. They made all the papers, sometimes twice in one day.

They were lured to the festival by the irrepressible Burton MacIntyre, the impresario of Whycocomagh.

"Fiona Hunter and I were lucky enough to be heard by Burton MacIntyre when we played on the open stage at Celtic Connections in Glasgow," says Fraya. "We did not win the competition, but something far more exciting came out of it. Burton approached us after our set and asked us how we would like to go to Celtic Colours. Silly question! Excited about this prospect, we kept in touch with Burton. Thanks to Burton's pushiness, the festival organizers decided to include us in the festival, giving us accommodation, amazing Canadian breakfasts (available at any time of night or day) and as many last-minute gigs as they could muster. All we had to do was raise the funds for our flights. Thanks to the Royal Scottish Academy of Music and Drama, where we studied at the time, and to local arts councils, we managed. We experienced Cape Breton square dancing, house ceilidhs, played at the Festival Club, in the interval on the opening night of the festival, on the radio, in a local university, and as warm-up act for Sharon Shannon's band, and Beòlach."

But it wasn't all perfect.

"Having forgotten about our early morning church performance, Fiona and I were partying away as is the custom at the Festival Club, when we were found by Burton and hurriedly escorted to the car for a long drive back to Whycocomagh. Whilst cruising the very wide roads home, I realized I had 'a call of nature.' Burton, not particularly amused with the state of us, abruptly stopped the car so that we could go outside. Fiona and I innocently sprawled out of the car to go pee in the ditch. Not realizing the width and depth of a Canadian ditch we went one step too far and just started falling . . . for what seemed like ages. We never did find the bottom. We struggled back up the harshly graded ditch and, precariously perched, got oor troos doon just in time for the police to turn up and ask if they could help!"

Back to the opening concert! The second half of that show introduced Irish-American fiddler Liz Carroll. With Tracey Dares-MacNeil on piano, Liz made the fiddle sing. Tracey was pregnant I think, and as busy as any other piano player that year.

Raylene Rankin of Cape Breton's famed Rankin Family, accompanied on guitar by Clarence Deveau, filled the arena as she sang songs in English and Gaelic, at one point inviting fiddler Mairi Rankin and piano player Mac Morin from Beòlach to join her on stage. Raylene ended her set with one of her greatest hits, Leon Dubinsky's "Rise Again," and the entire audience rose to their feet.

A standing ovation is a hard act to follow but Sharon Shannon was up to the challenge.

Introduced by Natalie MacMaster, she got great applause. "Hello everyone. How's it goin'? It's absolutely great to be back, we're deelighted to be back. Ahhmm. This is my sister Mary here. Mary Shannon on mandolin and banjo. And on the guitar, Jim Murray (mooray). From 'Macroon,' County Cork. Okay. We're gonna start with a tune (choon) that we learned from our (er) buddy (boody), Duncan (Dooncun) Chisholm."

She followed that with a tune learned off a recording by Jerry Holland, and finished off with a Carlos Núñez tune, thanking Phil Cunningham for fixing her accordion "or else we wouldn't even be able to do this tune. This one's for you Phil . . . ."

Sharon sat on stage in a semi-circle with her mandolin-playing sister Mary Shannon and guitarist Jim Murray and they went mad at the tunes. A beautifully sung song by Pauline Scanlon capped off the set and, had the show ended there, everyone would have left satisfied. But this is Celtic Colours, and the tunes were really just getting underway.

Masters of Ceremony Laurel Munroe, from the *Cape Breton Post*, and CBC Radio One host Ian McNeil returned to the stage to invite all the performers out for a grand finale. Cape Breton fiddler Howie MacDonald happened to be backstage so he joined the crowd on stage for a Gaelic song and a bunch of tunes. While Gillian Head was stepping it up centre stage, Howie spotted Rodney MacDonald—then Nova Scotia's Minister of Tourism and Culture, later its Premier—in the front row. Being a fiddler and a stepdancer himself, Rodney delighted all as he took Howie's invitation and joined him centre stage for a couple of steps.

"I was moved to tears twice last night," said Festival Director Max MacDonald. "It reminded me of why we do what we do. Sometimes you can get lost in the organization of it, but then the music makes it all worth it."

# Drivers are the heart of Celtic Colours.

One year, as Festival time approached, we packed up the office and moved out of our downtown Sydney office to set up shop at the Gaelic College. The Gaelic College campus turned out to serve us well as the centre of operations. Max called it "Festival Village." There were dorms for most of the artists and staff, space for offices and rehearsals, a cafeteria that served breakfast all night, and the Festival Club was on-site, open late and well within stumbling distance for festival artists and staff alike after a long hard day at work.

Our Production Office was a big room in MacLeod House, with Transportation taking up about half of the space. With long work tables lining two sides of the room, and huge charts on the walls above them—where all the information drivers needed could be seen at a glance—drivers knew who needed to be picked up, when, where and by whom.

Festival headquarters is a hub of activity. An army of volunteer drivers transports the hundreds of artists to communities all over the island to their shows, and back again to the Gaelic College. As the troops return each night, stories of how the shows went circulate quickly. The big buzz tonight is from Mabou where audiences were getting their first taste of Galician piper Carlos Núñez at the "Celtic Knot" concert. By all accounts, the audience was in rapture as the Galician piper defined the term world-class with a performance that added just the right touch of theatrics to the presentation of his music. Dressed in a white suit, Núñez's engaging presence attracts attention as if by force when he is on stage. Known the world over for his innovative and masterful playing, Carlos Núñez is one of Spain's most recognizable musicians. He has appeared on several Chieftains albums including the Grammy award-winning *Santiago*, and released four albums of his own, each one achieving platinum status for sales of 100,000 in Spain alone. But here, he was coming to Celtic Colours practically unknown.

Max MacDonald and Joella Foulds met Carlos several times at festivals in Scotland and Denmark where they discussed the possibility of his coming to Cape Breton. Finally, they were able to secure him, but they wanted something a little different.

"Usually, Carlos performs with a big band and dancers, and puts on a very extravagant show," explains MacDonald. "We wanted a more traditional line-up for Celtic Colours and Carlos agreed to a trio. But the trio turned into a duo of Carlos and his brother Xurxo when the third member of the trio couldn't make it at the last minute."

Carlos and Xurxo were quite a pair on stage. Carlos stood up straight with his pipes or whistles, precisely dressed, conducting with his body like dancing, designed to reach the back rows of a very big room. He's handsome, more hair hanging below his ears than above them, but like the girls used to say around the water cooler, "with eyes like that, he doesn't need any hair." His younger brother Xurxo also kept eyes glued to the stage, and not just for his outstanding musicianship, playing guitar and drums and percussion. He plays the stage like a cheerleader at a pep rally and it's never long before everyone's clapping along.

Carlos was very nervous at first but then thrilled at the reaction to his music and gained a new understanding that the music of his homeland could stand on its own in a different land. He discovered that Cape Breton reminded him of home in terms of importance of identity and music in culture. By the end of the festival, Carlos wanted to return to Celtic Colours. But in the spring, a new CD and a performance before 65,000 people in Paris on St. Patrick's Day led to a major tour of France, scheduled for October. Carlos promised he would be back for the Festival in 2004. Several weeks after that, however, he found out he was booked for another major European tour in October 2004. So Carlos called his manager immediately and said, "I cannot wait until 2005 to go back to Cape Breton. Cancel some of the French tour this year and see if they will have me at Celtic Colours."

"When the call came from Carlos' manager, we were thrilled and agreed immediately," said Joella Foulds.

But back to the drivers.

The drivers' brigade is definitely the sexiest of the volunteer corps. You get to meet the artists. You get to drive around in brand new rented vehicles. You become indispensable to the visiting artists. You must know your way around. Have a friendly, helpful disposition, and enjoy the company of others. You must not be the star-struck type or too chatty or pushy.

When speaking to artists about what they remember best about Celtic Colours, they always mention the drivers. And the breakfasts. But the drivers first. And faces light up and names come to mind, adventures are recalled, and then they start to ask, "How's Joe doing?" and "Jeez, you know, I haven't seen Byron in years," and "What's Stemer up to?" There's a genuine interest in catching up.

"The drivers become friends for life," says Corrina Hewat who has been coming to Celtic Colours since 1998. She praised the efforts of the drivers the year her mother and sister attended. "Just helping us get about and helping us buy things. Taking girls around and buying shoes, ya know? 'I wanna see a blue heron.' Nelson took me to see a blue heron."

David Milligan: "Occasionally you get looked after by somebody who's actually got a real passion for where they come from and their own culture—somebody who's like dying to show you everything—it's like, you've got to see this and you've got to see this. And the amazing thing about Cape Breton, particularly the drivers at that festival, is that there's never anything like 'uggghhh, gawd, ok.' It's all just kind of done very gently, very subtly, and if you've got time, if you've happened to have got out of your beds in time to leave a bit of spare time on the way to the gig, they'll show you something and it's truly amazing. And I think that's something that is very unique to the festival."

Gordie Campbell was Transportation Coordinator from 1998 to 2005. When he took over in 1998, there were thirty-three concerts and, except for one or two acts, the artists were staying in Baddeck. By 2002 there were forty-three concerts and, while most of the artists stayed in Gaelic College accommodations, there were some staying at hotels in Baddeck. The addition of ten shows over nine days was starting to tax the system Gordie had been using since he started, which was, frankly, to make it up as he went along, based on the very solid foundation laid by his predecessor Gail Holdner.

"The system was in my head," Gordie said. "As mad as it may seem, we would know ahead of time what the flights were for arrivals and departures for the foreign artists or anyone coming into Cape Breton, so we knew when the pickups were in Halifax or Sydney airports. And we knew where the concerts were, and the soundchecks were laid out, and we had a book and that was all laid out. And I could basically do the timelines for the festival according to that. And equipment moves maybe a little later on. And slight changes for that.

"So it was mapped out on a timeline and on a spreadsheet, but it was always changing, so that eventually—and I don't know who came up with the idea at the time—but to put everything on huge sheets of paper, and just paste it on the walls. So everybody could look up and could know what was happening; every volunteer could come in and see what was happening two, three, four days ahead of time. And a lot of times, somebody who was not really involved in the planning process would come up and highlight a problem or highlight a solution to a problem and that's how we did it. It was very communally done."

Once the festival is underway, there is great energy in the Production Office. The drivers' area is a constant hub of activity—coming and going, picking up assignments and dropping off keys, chasing after artists who have typically just gone out the other door, or checking the schedule to confirm where they're going next and who they're picking up. Site and stage managers pass through, checking in. And reporters and photographers come through for their media kits.

It's usually the first stop for visiting artists. Their designated driver takes them directly to the office to get sorted out with welcome kits, bracelets, room keys and meal tickets. They wander back to ask more questions, look for someone or something they've lost, or to just hang around.

"There was great *craic*," remembered Nuala Kennedy, who spent a lot of time in the Production Office. "Just hanging out with the drivers. It was deadly. They had a CD player, and they had a few drinks and stuff for us at night, when they were off duty and we didn't have a show. I was over there a lot. They were all so friendly and into the music and everything."

And busy. While the office did tend to get a little more social later in the evenings, as Festival Club time approached, there was always plenty of work to do. In more recent years, there wasn't as much of a gathering in the office. It was still a welcoming and social place, but renovations in the building reduced the space to half the size. It was well worth it for the upgrades, but it meant there was not as much room in the office for pastimes like Artists in Residence Office Chair Races and late-night "indoor football," as Fraya Thomsen described it. But the space was plenty big enough for us to function. And we functioned well.

Each day's soundchecks start between two and three in the afternoon, and each act has a set amount of time scheduled to get set up and work out any problems with the Tech Crew—the sound and light technicians who get everything looking and sounding professional. So musicians have to be at each venue on time, and we have to maintain the soundcheck schedule. Otherwise, the next act would have to wait or, worse, they'd run out of time to get the soundchecks done before the show.

Depending on where the concert is, departure time for soundchecks could be as early as noon. When we need to get someone to Port Morien or D'Escousse or even Big Pond, it's sometimes a scramble in the morning. Sometimes artists have to double- or triple-up on the rides, depending on their numbers and the equipment that has to be transported. And if it's one of those concerts where a crowd of musicians will be on stage, all performing at the same time—like "The New Tunemakers" concert in 2007, or "Tunes Gu Lèor" in 2009—everybody will be required on site for the soundcheck. When that happens, a caravan takes off all at once, and it's a race against the clock.

Gordie Campbell told me: "Each year, Transportation got bigger and bigger. I didn't have anything to go on. It had to be done. And there was a really strong team of people who came on board. Celtic Colours was very lucky in the fact that we had some people in the area that were skilled and also had a huge passion for what was going on, who would come and work on the Festival. People like Nigel Kearns and Shauna Walters and Gail Holdner and many others who came on board, and they all linked together very strongly as a team. So that if anybody wanted something or needed something, the other person would do it for them. It was just developing as it went. We'd get together and meet two months ahead of time. Max would sit down and say this is what we're doing. I would start making the preliminary plans of what had to be done, a budget, how we'd have to increase our resources, gas, or if we need more drivers, or how many vehicles we'd need. I'd map that out and put it back to the directors and then they would go out and find sponsorship for that. And it was just like a big chess game.

"We were responsible for the transportation side of basically everything. Which was picking artists up wherever they were and running them around the Festival, soundchecks and whatever happens. We'd also be responsible for moving all the sound equipment, moving all the technical side, all the backline, instruments, water, food—anybody wanted anything, we had to get it there.

"We had to create full concerts at the rink in Baddeck. We had to bring in 1500 chairs. Tables. Staging. Everything had to be created for that show. On the logistics side of it, it was just down to myself and volunteers to coordinate that and make it all happen and there was a huge strong body of volunteers and I can't say it enough that the volunteers—they're the ones who did it all. A lot of people would take on responsibility for certain events and they would coordinate that. It evolved from there. Certain people, their skills came outwards and they got more involved as the years went on. And that carried on to when I left, eight years later, that three volunteers—Blair Brown, Donnie MacAulay and Gerardette Brown—kind of took over my place."

Gordie is a man whose life has been changed by Celtic Colours. "That's where I met my wife. That's why I live in Scotland. First day we met, she came up to me and said, 'I hear you're the man who can get me a bass.' And I got her a double bass . . . ."

Gordie went on: "It's amazing stuff that goes on. I got to witness a fair bit of that. Blazin' Fiddles, backstage, my wife at the time was in the band and two of the members of the band were fairly young and it was their first time at the festival. It was the first year at the Gaelic College and Sean McGuire was an infinitely famous character, an Irish fiddle player with a reputation for being a cantankerous man, and backstage he was sitting in a corner and no one was paying attention to him and he asked to borrow a fiddle off one of the Blazin' Fiddles, Aidan O'Rourke, and Aidan just said, 'No.' Like, 'I don't know who you are old man,' which, at this point, Sean had had a tracheotomy and so he put his finger over the hole and basically said, like, 'Get me my fiddle and I'll show these little bastards what I can do.' He had no intention of playing that evening, but just because of that banter he put on an amazing 45-minute set, on the stage. Just amazing. And they still tell the story of what went on. And this is all part of the Festival. This is why we all got involved in the Festival. The energy levels. Just to be part of the interaction of all these things. You know, as a person in the audience you don't get to see all this stuff and just because you are a part of it you got to see amazing things. Amazing things. It will live with you forever."

Aidan O'Rourke told me that same story: "Well it was late. Blazers were warming up. Myself and Iain MacFarlane were lashing through some reels. Really flying. Fueled Cape Breton style. We were younger then." Aidan laughed. "The tunes were just flowing out of us. A few people had gathered. Out of the corner of my eye I caught a glimpse of an older gentleman. It was Sean McGuire staring at me. Really eyeballing me and my fiddle. I kept going for a while and the tunes died down. Still staring at me he marched over and barked at me, 'Give me that fiddle, boy!' I handed it to him. Without blinking he flew into his hit, 'The Mason's Apron,' with variations. We just stood agog! He went right through the whole thing. Twice. Then he stopped, nodded, and still staring, handed me the fiddle back, and marched off."

Gordie Campbell again: "Max and Joella were very smart at the start of the festival. Being both musicians and artists themselves, they knew the important thing is to take care of the musicians. The drivers weren't just somebody hired to do a job. If you took care of the musicians they'd give double on the stage, and that's just the ethos of Celtic Colours and it continues. And the artists will always go away with positive stories. And spread the word about Cape Breton and the Festival around the world.

"Donnie MacAulay and Blair Brown have done a great job of continuing out of the year I left—out of that ethos of the drivers getting together as a group. Working together from that, they formed an association and that association does fundraising. Each year, that money makes possible the recording of a Cape Breton artist. I'm very proud of that ethos of them working together and doing something for the music around the year, and not just during Celtic Colours."

Gerardette Brown remembers a concert one night. "Transportation Coordinator Gordie Campbell needed an extra driver for the 'Step Into the Past' concert at Fortress of Louisbourg. My passengers were a famous storyteller and Gaelic singer from Scotland—Margaret Bennett—and a trio from Québec billed as Marchand, Ornstein and Miron.

"It was a rainy, windy cold night, as usual in Louisbourg. I had to stop in the main village to buy umbrellas for our walk to the King's Bastion. The rain was torrential. The musicians had a short soundcheck, then we walked through the cobblestone street down to one of the eighteenth-century restaurants where a meal was being served for the artists, the volunteers, and the patrons who paid ninety dollars for this first-class show, eighteenth-century style. The French trio asked me to join them at their table and, in the fortress tradition, I served the soup.

"My guests were speaking French, but I could pick up a few words and expressions, as my grandmother was Acadian. One of the group, accordion player Normand Miron, was obviously concerned by something. My first thought was my driving, as the wind and the rain might have made them nervous. The woman member of the group, Lisa, told me in English that Normand wanted to know if Louisbourg was a military establishment. I gave a brief history of the Fortress of Louisbourg and joked how the Cape Breton fort was built to protect the passage to Québec. The young man went on to say that after his soundcheck, he went to the men's washroom at the King's Bastion. He was at the bathroom sink and thought he was alone, until he saw in the mirror the ghost of an eighteenth-century soldier standing behind him.

"I didn't pay much attention—my concern was walking in the dark back to the chapel where the concert would be held. I was put at ease later that evening during the show when Lisa congratulated the government on the restoration of Louisbourg and the importance of retaining our history. The ghost must have been proud to hear that!"

Some of our drivers go above and beyond. Frank Sampson left early afternoon for the Halifax Airport, picked up his artist and headed back to Baddeck, usually a ten-hour day. This trip had at least three extra stops along the way back for "health breaks," so he was just a little behind schedule. One commitment the drivers make is to cover the back shift or the 11 p.m. to 7 a.m. Festival Club drive. Artists that play or party at the Club that stay in Baddeck require a drive home. Frank returned from that very long trip and, seeing that there was no other driver to cover, stayed on to make sure the artists got back to their hotel that nigh—er—morning.

Gerardette and Blair Brown tell a story of the Middle River Square Dance. "Joella and Max wanted us to try our hand at site and stage managing. Our assignment was the Middle River Community Hall. It was the last Friday night of the festival and the night before the Great Big Square Dance in Baddeck. Just before heading down to the hall, Joella told us there was a possibility Burton MacIntyre would not be able to attend the dance to be the prompter, but she was making alternate arrangements. The venue volunteers were most hospitable, even though there had been a death in the community that day. They were short-handed, but we reassured them we were there to help. To put the rest of this story into perspective: there is a lot of square dance politics and etiquette in Cape Breton. There are Sydney sets, Inverness sets, Baddeck sets, etc., and this night was no exception. Joella's replacement prompter was from Virginia and had taken part in the festival's workshops, demonstrating contra dancing. Rather than letting the square dance take the natural route, and starting on the participants' terms, the guest prompter had other plans—'Let's introduce contra dancing.'

"Some people took her challenge, but most of the locals were still seated. To put things mildly, some of the patrons came right up to our faces and demanded the organizers were going to hear from them! They came to dance, not to attend a workshop! To top that, during one set the prompter told the fiddler to 'slow it down a bit'!

"One thing you don't tell a fiddler is to slow it down.

"We had to defuse the situation, and Blair asked her politely, explaining the customer was always right, to honour their request to dance. The prompter obliged—for a while. Just when things were starting to pick up, she was back on stage giving directions. The dance floor cleared.

"Time to call reinforcements. Blair took the cell phone—the only mandatory tool of a driver at that time—and tried to get Max or Joella, before the patrons did. Cell phone reception wasn't the best out in the woods, but Blair walked around the parking lot along the road's edge, found a signal, it faded, but he kept walking. He got in touch with Max. Max told Blair, 'Stay where you are, I can hear you clearly.' Blair asked Max to talk fast, as he was standing in the middle of the highway on the centre line. Max agreed the prompter had to be told that the local audience was more important. They shall have their dance, without a prompter.

"The show carried on, and the dancers danced. Blair and I helped the locals to tidy and close the hall. The artist had a good time, but we were both devastated. We were sure our assignment had failed and we wouldn't be asked back to another festival. When we returned to the office, both Max and Joella apologized for the snafu. Fellow volunteers who were experienced in site and stage management were supportive, saying we were the best to handle the situation. Have we site and stage managed since? NO! Give us airport runs, scattered artists to round up, and rainy-windy nights to drive in any day!"

### A Day in the Life of a Celtic Colours Driver

| | |
|---|---|
| 12:00 a.m. | Stop drinking (drivers have an obligation to refrain from drinking 12 hours before they are scheduled to drive). |
| 1:00 a.m. | Eat breakfast. |
| 1:30 a.m. | Find the drivers' quiet room. |
| 1:35 a.m. | Select an unused bed. |
| 9:00 a.m. | Eat breakfast! (Yes, again) Catch up on gossip from previous night. |
| 10:00 a.m. | Report to Transportation Office—review assignment with coordinators. Van or car Passengers |

Pick-up location—Gaelic College/Baddeck hotel
Destination—community/venue
Soundcheck time 2:15 p.m. (any leeway??!!)
Complete sign-out sheets: credit card, radio/cell phone, vehicle/keys
Get water
Locate artists
Report to pick up CDs/floats/paperwork
Locate artists
Don't forget the water
Wait for artists (having breakfast)

| | |
|---|---|
| 11:30 a.m. | Check vehicle for cleanliness and fuel |
| 11:45 a.m. | Get artists in van (fondly referred to as herding the chickens) |
| 11:50 a.m. | Get water |
| 11:55 a.m. | Get artists back in van (kittens back in the box) |
| 12:00 p.m. | Check with coordinators for changes or updates—pick up piano at Festival Club |
| 12:05 p.m. | Get artists back in van |
| 12:10 p.m. | Driver radios to base station with confirmation "We're on the road!" |
| 12:15 p.m. | Become the Cape Breton tour guide/ambassador/historian |
| 1:00 p.m. | Artists request bathroom break (preferably close to "refreshment stand") |
| 2:00 p.m. | Arrive at venue—introduce to site and stage volunteers and ensure everything is set for the artists |
| 2:15 p.m. | Artists' soundcheck started (ON TIME!) |
| 2:30 p.m. | Meet with venue volunteers for set-up area for CD sales |
| 3:00 p.m. | Find local refreshment stand (under obligation to serve the artists) |
| 2:45-5:00 p.m. | Driver attempts to enjoy performance by various artists and technical wizardry! Attends to artists' needs and desires, such as picking up supplies/gifts, etc. at local stores, e.g., new shirt or jeans for tonight's shows. Also assists as required at venue with various duties such as putting up posters, signage, etc. Other duties as assigned. |
| 5:00 p.m. | Dines with artists and other drivers and volunteers at the venue-sponsored meal (anything from sandwiches to deep-fried turkey or eighteenth-century feast) |
| 6:00 p.m. | Meet with all the show's artists to set up sales of their CDs—sign forms, arrange display (Can I see the show from here???) |
| 7:30 p.m. | Show begins . . . . |

8:30 p.m.  Intermission—sell CDs (Watch for shoplifters. Did I give too much change? Was that an empty CD case? Sorry, no credit cards or debit! Is that song on this CD?)

10:00 p.m.  Show ends. As audience leaves—sell more CDs. Count CDs. Count money. Settle with artist. Count money again. Ensure all forms are complete.

11:00 p.m.  Get artists in van . . . .

11:05 p.m.  Thank community volunteers

11:10 p.m.  Get artists back in van

11:15 p.m.  Radio to home base: All aboard and accounted for! Heading for home.        Er . . . Sorry, the Red Shoe!

12:00 a.m.  Arrive at Red Shoe!

1:00 a.m.  Head home with new lifetime friends. Radio to base. Concentrate on driving above snoring!

2:00 a.m.  Arrive at home base. Turn in keys, credit card, radio, cell phone

2:15 a.m.  Settle with CD office. Exchange stories of the day with other drivers.

2:30 a.m.  Check Transportation Board for next assignment

2:35 a.m.  On it! Breakfast, then to bed!

2:35 a.m.  Not on it! Festival Club!

# There was no hiding it. Or denying it.

I was still a little tipsy. I could tell by the way I tripped over a couple of words on the first phone call I got—the one that woke me up and sent me out to my desk to start the day.

To be fair, I was sound asleep in my bed, probably not long after having had breakfast with a typical Cape Breton crew who played earlier that night and then led a huge session onstage at the Festival Club until an hour or so after they stopped serving liquor. So it got late pretty early that night and before very long at all, it was getting bright.

I thought something like this might happen and worked late myself to make sure I was covered for the morning, and if things went as planned, into the early afternoon. Sometimes you get a little spot, during all the chaos, that you can just kinda chill. It never lasts long, and you have to be very careful not to step out of the bubble—once I had to go to a show in Sydney and I made the mid-week, rookie-ish-in-retrospect, mistake of stopping at my apartment and having a hot bath in the big old claw-foot tub. It was hard to come back from that one.

Now it's just after one o'clock in the afternoon, and I'm sitting at my desk, staring at my computer, trying to get my head around what I do have to do today. First things first though. Gotta get to the cafeteria in time for a bite to eat before they close for the day. That's one of the hardest things to get used to during Celtic Colours—managing to eat.

The cafeteria at the Gaelic College, where the festival has been headquartered since 2000, keeps the strangest hours. It opens at 1 a.m. with a breakfast menu that includes boiled, fried or scrambled eggs; bacon, ham or sausage; hash browns (of the deep-fried potato cube variety); white or whole-wheat toast; and a fruit cup. I think there's a French toast option as well. And apple or orange juice. On a normal day (or night, depending on how you look at it), the cafeteria serves most of its breakfasts between 2 a.m. and 6 a.m., as people are on their way to bed after a late night at the Festival Club. At around 11 a.m. they start to serve daytime food too, which includes a choice of soup and sandwich or a hot meal. And then at 2 p.m., they close for the day. So if you sleep too late, or get tied up with work, you could easily miss food completely.

After a quick check of my e-mails, printing off a couple that I can read over breakfast, and a glance at my to-do list for the day, I grab my sunglasses and head out into the overcast day for the thirty-second walk to the cafeteria in MacKenzie Hall—ya gotta keep in shape!

I've got my Celtic Colours souvenir water bottle to fill up at the water cooler. Water before coffee on "mornings" like this. One thing I've learned over the years is that hydration is very important. The coffee is for after eating, heading back to sit at my desk in the Production Office. And I've taken to mixing it with hot chocolate and some cream to make it just a little more like a treat rather than a necessity.

The cafeteria is sparsely populated this time of day. There are a few late-rising artists grabbing a bite before they head out to their soundcheck, some looking a little worse for the wear. And I can relate, having been sitting with them in this same room as few as five hours ago.

There are a couple of drivers hanging around chatting, reading the *Cape Breton Post*, a stack of which were dropped off earlier. They're waiting for their musicians to get it together so they can hit the road. I usually try to find a place by myself to eat and look over the newspaper to see what's been written about the festival, read a few e-mails and get my own head together about what's on the go for this day. Plus, my phone is likely to ring at any minute with some sort of emergency.

A couple of grilled cheese sandwiches before they close for the day is the winner. I'd had breakfast a couple of hours earlier, before I went to bed, so I was in no need of eggs and bacon at this point, and the shepherd's pie they had as a hot food option looked good, but seemed like a heavy way to start the day.

Back on the phone now, explaining how the media accreditation process works to a blogger I had never heard from before who wanted to videotape a couple of concerts for her website, starting tonight.

It was a reasonable enough request. If only I'd gotten it sooner. Usually my schedule was flexible enough that I could meet media folk who made unexpected requests at the last minute, but that year I was tied up on a week-long project that was requiring my day-long presence at a different venue most of the week. And she needed media accreditation in order to be videotaping. And there would have to be releases signed by the artists. And what about sound? Unfortunately, none of our locations were going to match up.

I sometimes wonder if she shot some video anyway. I never did hear about it if she did.

It's not like these issues couldn't be dealt with on site without my being there. We have a consistently great team of technicians, site and stage managers, and community volunteers. But I have found that things go wrong more often when I can't get to a show being covered by media who have never been to the festival, or who I have never met. Especially with video.

There's a lot more to getting good video than just standing there shooting, out of the way at the back of the room. And shooting from your seat can be disruptive. But there's no point in them being there if they can't get their shots, and getting their shots can sometimes be an invasive process. Sometimes it's just not worth it.

But oh—for a break. Even if it's just lying in your bunk with the radio on and nothing to do and nowhere to be for a couple of hours. You can't actually sleep, but you can kind of relax a little and not think about anything but what's on the radio. Until the phone rings.

On a beautiful day at another Celtic Colours venue in St. Ann's, the sound of fiddles and piano fills the air as "The Thriving Cape

Breton Fiddle" show is underway across the Gaelic College campus at the Great Hall of the Clans. The sun is shining, artists with the day off are lounging about the grounds, hanging out and catching up with friends who've just arrived. Sitting around a picnic table under a great big tree outside MacKenzie Hall, Kris Drever, Nuala Kennedy and Alasdair Codona are discussing their first impressions of the festival.

"Bumping into lots of people you know but don't often get to see is one of the best things about this festival," says Kris Drever, who plays guitar with Fine Friday, a group that includes flute-player Nuala Kennedy and fiddler Anna-Wendy Stevenson. He is still raving about the show last night at Englishtown. "It was a brilliant gig. The audience was really good, really cheerful and friendly."

Alasdair Codona—a talented and versatile singer of Gaelic songs—agrees with Drever, speaking of how he feels connected to the people here: "I enjoy playing the ceilidhs, in a way, more than the big shows. I played at Englishtown the last time I was here and the people remember you. It's not like you're a big star on a big stage and there's this separation between you and the audience. It's more like you are welcomed into a community."

Alasdair was also very pleased with the workshops he's been doing, speaking highly of "The Gaelic Song" workshop yesterday afternoon in Johnstown. He excitedly described the old waulking board, the likes of which he'd never seen, that made its way to Johnstown from Scotland, and he observed delightedly how little the Canadian accent has influenced the local Gaelic, finding instead great similarities to accents from Barra and Uist.

"It's a beautiful place," continues Kris Drever, who comes from Orkney, a group of islands off the northern coast of Scotland, and who had never been to Cape Breton Island before.

Jens Jacobsen and Ulla Posselt are also visiting Cape Breton for the first time, on vacation from Denmark where they both volunteer for the Tønder Festival. Ulla, who takes care of artist accommodations at Tønder, is quick to praise the volunteers here at Celtic Colours, especially the drivers.

"They take care of the artists very well. They are very knowl-edgeable and know about the music." This is a point Nuala Kennedy is quick to pick up on. "They really have time to look after the artists," says Nuala, sporting the new pants she picked up when one of the drivers took her shopping after her luggage got delayed on the transatlantic journey to Cape Breton.

So that year's festival is on. Nine shows down, thirty-five to go. Late nights at the Festival Club are starting to take hold. It's break-fast before bedtime again.

"It must be hard to sleep with all that music going on."

"Sleep?"

There's not much time for sleep, or interest in sleeping and missing something, as we approach the middle of the festival and artists continue to arrive. Last night the lads from Irish band Danú, a festival favourite, showed up—unscheduled and unexpected—at the Festival Club. They had a night off from their tour, so they decided to drop in on their way from New Brunswick to Pictou, which isn't on the way at all. They took the stage by storm, much to the delight of the crowd overflowing the Great Hall of the Clans, and were hardly allowed to leave when they'd finished their tunes.

It was another night of stealing applause at the Festival Club. Just as an act was finished onstage and the crowd ready to erupt in applause, Phil Cunningham—who wasn't playing—would make his way to the middle of the dance floor in front of the stage and graciously accept the audience's praise with a deeply exaggerated bow. This delighted whomever was on stage in a "ya cheeky bastard" kind of way, and the joke grew funnier each time he repeated it, occasionally joined by other merry-making festival artists.

Ask anyone who frequented the club about Phil Cunningham's keyboard interpretation of "Danny Boy." Phil finds his way onstage. He seats himself behind the piano and starts into that old Irish favourite. Phil's rendition has the entire, standing-room-only Hall of the Clans in an uproar as he seems to struggle with the well-known classic, misplacing a finger here, adding an inappropriate flourish there. So he goes on, gaining confidence with the tune's familiarity, then embellishing with over-confidence, visibly quite proud of himself for having figured it out, smiling over-smugly as he reaches for the next chord and fumbles again, repeating the process to great effect. The musicians in the audience are first to get the joke that has the musicians onstage trying to keep a straight face, but breaking up into uproarious laughter. The musicians in the crowd start to chuckle with each over-confident mistake and end up bent over, practically falling over each other in laughter. The assorted festival patrons catch on as Phil searches for notes that aren't there, finds ones that shouldn't be. By now it is obvious that he is hamming it up, as obvious as the triumphant look on his face, and the look of despair that replaces it as his miscalculated risks with the melody go horribly wrong.

Other outstanding sets included the French-Canadian trio of guitarist André Marchand, fiddler Lisa Ornstein and hurdy-gurdy player Normand Miron. The three members of this group used to play together in the influential band La Bottine Souriante. Their sound is typically Québécois, with the feet used as percussion. They draw on a rich history of music from the nineteenth-century immigration of the Irish and Scottish and their assimilation into Québec culture through intermarriage. The influence of these immigrants' music on an already fiddle-rich tradition of French music is a hallmark of traditional Québécois music. They demonstrated all this in a set of the tunes, animated by Normand Miron, whose sense of humour needs no translation from his limited command of the English language.

There were sessions in the Green Room so full that there was hardly enough elbow room to tip a glass of drink. Some of the overflow landed back at one of the residences for another session with the guys from Danú, Sharon Shannon's band, Duncan Chisholm, Cape Bretoners Paul Cranford, Paul MacDonald and Dave Papazian, Danish fiddler Tove de Fries, British Columbian Daniel Lapp on trumpet and assorted others.

Suddenly, it was bright outside the window, bright enough to turn off the lamps in the room and head for breakfast before bed. Again. It may be autumn, but around here the days are getting longer.

By mid-week, it's starting to feel like we've lost a day somewhere. It was bound to happen, endless nights of music, busy days of logistics, people constantly coming and going. Twenty-nine shows in six days, fifteen left to go. Daydreaming of sleep. Can't complain though.

One year, on the stage at Centre 200, a carefully-kilted Phil Cunningham closed the first half of the show accompanied on fiddle by an equally kilted Duncan Chisholm and a sharply-suited Malcolm Stitt on guitar.

"I've never tried this before," starts Cunningham, "a kilt on stage." The audience laughs as he tries to make himself comfortable, sitting on stage—the surface of which is approximately eye-level for the seated audience—with his accordion strapped to his chest. "My mum has always wanted me to come onstage wearing my kilt, but I'm telling ya, this is the first time . . . and the last. I just don't know how to be . . . ." Again the audience laughs out loud as he shifts uncomfortably in his chair, trying not to give the first few rows more of a show than they had bargained for. "You're laughing, eh?" Cunningham almost sounds hurt. "It's alright for you, you're in the dark," he tells the crowd. "You don't have a big spotlight shining up your dress."

The laughter dies down as the trio eases into a set of tunes that starts with accordion and fiddle. Malcolm Stitt picks at chords on the guitar and the notes seep into the tune, making their presence known in the scant space between the notes and tones of the accordion and fiddle. It really is a beautiful sound—a fitting combination of instruments and just the right musicians to bring it to life.

**As the result of a hectic Media Relations mission, I found myself one night at the Louisbourg Playhouse just in time to catch a concert.**

I was there to meet a German television crew, but they hadn't arrived yet, so I stayed for the concert. Celtic Colours "Louisbourg Crossroads" recognizes that Louisbourg has been a cultural crossroads for almost 400 years. At the Crossroads that year I got to hear Edinburgh, Scotland-based trio Fine Friday, British Columbian fiddler and trumpet player Daniel Lapp with United Kingdom guitarist Ian Carr and the Cape Breton fiddle, piano, bass combo of Kimberley Fraser, Stephanie Wills and Allie Bennett.

Multiple standing ovations only begin to tell the story of the concert I saw that night. Kimberley Fraser, known as "one of Cape Breton's finest up-and-coming fiddlers," opened the show accompanied by Wills on piano and Bennett on guitar and bass. Kimberley is a fiddler—and piano player and stepdancer—whose name came up in a lot of conversations at Celtic Colours. Tours with Cherish the Ladies and trips to major festivals like Tønder Festival were still ahead for Fraser, but at seventeen it was obvious on that night that there was a bright future for this talented Northside native. It was clear to the audience, anyway, as her set ended with the first standing ovation of the night.

Fine Friday followed with a playful set of tunes and a song. This trio represents a crossroads in itself. They came together from different groups playing in sessions around Edinburgh, an enlightened city known for fostering an environment for the intermingling of musical ideas. Their line-up of Irish-born flute player and singer Nuala Kennedy, fiddler Anna-Wendy Stevenson from Edinburgh and guitarist and singer Kris Drever of Orkney, Scotland, neatly weaves melody and harmony. And when it's over, the audience stands in appreciation, slack-jawed and clapping their hands.

After intermission, Daniel Lapp and Ian Carr took the stage. Daniel led the way on trumpet and fiddle with tunes and a song or two, and stories about the tunes. He introduced a unique bowing style that involved loosening the hairs on the bow, laying the bowhair across the strings with the bow going under the neck, and taking the ends of the bowhair in his bowing hand. It produces a drone-like sound, in some ways not unlike a hurdy-gurdy. When he bows, he gets all four strings every time so he uses chords. He admits that although he did think of this technique—it came to him in a dream—he isn't the only one using it. He used the technique to accompany his singing of a lovely Richard Thompson song. He topped it with yet another version of "Danny Boy," playing trumpet and fiddle and singing while Ian played guitar. After a raft of tunes, it was another standing ovation.

And then the finale when everyone piled on stage: Ian and Kris on guitar, Nuala with the flute, Anna-Wendy and Kimberley and Daniel playing fiddles, Stephanie on piano and Allie on bass and/or fiddle. A cultural crossroads meeting in the common traditional music of the east and west coasts of Canada. And then the standing ovation. And then the encore. And another standing ovation. As commonplace as it may seem, the standing ovation is really quite a remarkable thing. What is it about music that can move a crowd of people, strangers—albeit ones with a common interest—to the point of jumping out of their seats, hooting and whooping and clapping their hands?

People talked for days about button accordion player Joe Derrane at the Festival Club on his last night, having just crossed the island after his gig in Chéticamp. Here he was with Frankie Gavin on fiddle and Brian McGrath on the piano. Joe must be in his 70s and he had to give 'er up years ago—now he's back at it and loving it and playing like he's blessed to have it back in his hands. And the audience felt it, whether in that beautiful slow one or the one that made you wanna dance.

And to further wow the Festival Club, Dwayne Côté came from his concert with Maybelle Chisholm MacQueen at "West Meets East" in St. Peters, to join Sheumas MacNeil and Paul MacDonald, piano and guitar.

It's farewell to André Marchand, Lisa Ornstein and Normand Miron who headed out in the dark of night, but not before Lisa answered the oft-asked question, "Did you have a good time?" with "It was the best festival I've ever been to."

And it was sad to see Sharon Shannon and her band drive away to the airport Wednesday afternoon. Having the combination of Sharon and her band housed with Phil Cunningham, Duncan Chisholm, Malcolm Stitt and Éamonn Coyne for even a couple of days is worth all the organizational effort, providing just the right touches to allow them to play music with people they know, admire, and respect. And they certainly took advantage of that chance, playing together well into the morning most nights, exchanging tunes and ideas in a way that they rarely get.

The life of a professional, touring musician—especially artists in demand—is a hectic one. It's usually one-off shows, traveling all over the place. Here, at the Celtic Colours Festival, they are all in one place for a couple of days and that creates a little musical bubble. But they are now on their way.

Tom Knapp: "We witnessed some incredible pick-up bands that came out of the musicians' backstage interactions. On one night, the club closed down with an unbroken forty-minute blast featuring local fiddlers Troy MacGillivray, Andrea Beaton and Joe Peter MacLean, plus Sheumas MacNeil on piano, John Ferguson on guitar, Cheryl Smith on drums and Daniel Lapp on trumpet.

"So vigorous was the music, a few dozen members of the crowd couldn't resist a ragged but tireless square set that continued till nearly 4 a.m.

"We saw Sharon Shannon excitedly swapping shoes with several members of the crowd at the edge of the Festival Club stage. Saw her touring singer, Pauline Scanlon, trade shoes and shirts with one of the guys.

"We saw up-and-comer Cynthia MacLeod from Prince Edward Island, playing her fiddle with a grin so wide I feared her cheeks might crack, kicking off from the stage with both feet so fiercely I half expected her to take off.

"We watched Kendra MacGillivray, Troy MacGillivray and Dave MacIsaac toss around a lengthy stream of melodies while Sabra MacGillivray showed off her dancing excellence. Sabra is virtually inexhaustible and has steps so fresh I think she must be inventing them on the spot. Later that evening, she told me that she sometimes is. Meanwhile, Kendra continued to drive the music forward with unparalleled energy, closing out the set by jumping to her feet and joining her sister in the dance.

"Unfortunately, one year festival organizers decided to crack down on participants, forbidding anyone who wasn't on the festival payroll from playing in sessions. That was disappointing news to a lot of local and visiting musicians who enjoyed the casual interaction and the chance to play with the "stars." Many touring performers also expressed disappointment in the new rule, noting that they enjoyed the chance to sit back and listen to other people jam for a while, joining in as the spirit moved them. The new mandate prohibited them from inviting friends and acquaintances to the jam.

"Sadly, some organizers need to be reminded that music lives best in a fluid, communal environment. Strict regulations governing who can play when and where are fine in a concert setting, but it stifles the purpose of a session."

There is a reason for this "crackdown" and it has to do with what we've come to call "session busters," those beginners who insist on being in on the session with "the stars" even though there is little chance they will be able to keep up.

"In any case, music won't be denied, and many people got around the new restrictions by seeking entertainment elsewhere. Some folks went back to congregating and jamming in the dormitory lobby. I didn't hear any complaints about the noise this year, and the music was grand! Others were invited to join the excitement at outside locales, such as the big Belle Côte hoopla that ran for more than ten hours on a government tab, and a party that ran past sunrise one morning at the MacNeil home—parents of the Barra MacNeils—in Sydney Mines."

In our seventh year, the calibre of the production left many in the audience commenting that the opening show was the best ever. The combination of such internationally recognized acts as Natalie MacMaster, Carlos Núñez and Lúnasa would have been an impressive enough show, but the production of the concert itself was also designed to impress. The production included big screens on either side of the stage, amplifying the onstage action with close-ups from two hand-held cameras working the stage. It was the brainchild of Technical Director Nigel Kearns.

We saw in one day that high standard maintained through half a dozen concerts in Whycocomagh, Big Pond, Bras d'Or, Inverness, New Waterford, and Petit-de-Grat. A beautiful afternoon of "Pastoral Airs" at St. Matthew's Church in Inverness led to an evening of outstanding performances all over the map. In New Waterford, pianist Doug MacPhee hosted some living legends of Cape Breton fiddling—Buddy MacMaster, John Campbell and Carl MacKenzie. Big Pond's Gordie Sampson, Cape Breton's fiddling funny man Howie MacDonald, and one of the hits from opening night, Lúnasa, kept a full house in Sampson's home community entertained with a night of songs and tunes. Carlos Núñez continued to dazzle audiences with his performance in Whycocomagh where A Crowd of Bold Sharemen from Newfoundland picked up their instruments and added to their growing reputation as the best of the best contemporary traditional groups from Newfoundland. Beòlach, Dave Gunning and Patricia Murray lived up to the accolades following each of them around with winning performances in Bras d'Or.

And that one day's late-night Festival Club swung into high

gear with a smoking performance by Beòlach and the ever-generous Carlos Núñez sharing the stage with Rear Boisdale fiddler Joe Peter MacLean—the man about whom Gaelic storyteller Joe Neil MacNeil once said, "That fellow could get music out of a stone."

A favourite concert every year is the annual "Step Into the Past" concert at the Fortress of Louisbourg. This candle-lit meal-and-concert is always the first to sell out. An early driving assignment had introduced me to this rare concert, and to the beauty and surprising versatility of harp playing.

We arrived in the afternoon, Corrina Hewat and Laoise Kelly with me as designated driver. Ardyth Robinson and Jennifer Wyatt—a harp duo from Halifax—followed us from Baddeck in their own car, around to the back entrance of the Fortress of Louisbourg National Historic Park.

After we crossed the moat of bleating sheep and goats, we entered the old chapel in the King's Bastion. Soundcheck was relatively simple as it would be an acoustic show and therefore no PA—which was convenient since the place didn't have electricity, being a reconstruction of an eighteenth-century building. The only worry was that Laoise's harp wouldn't show up on time. They had neglected to put it on her flight from Ireland.

This was the performers' first meeting and they negotiated a set list over dinner, trying to get the right mix of fast and slow numbers. Dinner was by candlelight, of course, and consisted of vegetable soup served in pewter bowls, salmon, rice, carrots, wine, dessert, tea and coffee.

The audience was paraded into the chapel by candlelight. On the altar were four harps, flanked by candelabras. The closeness of the crowd was starting to warm up the unheated room. Dozens of candles cast shadowy light as Rosemary MacCormack opened the program with a reading of poetry by Scottish harpist Fiona Davidson, gently underscored by Corrina Hewat on harp. MacCormack continued in Gaelic, setting the tone and introducing the show.

Jennifer and Ardyth sang in harmony, accompanied by a single harp, or played delicate melodies together. Their rendition of "Mist Covered Mountains," as a duet, replaced the chorus with a series of whole notes which, given the appropriate rhythm, would sound Mi'kmaq.

The idea of harp music conjures up a serene image. Jennifer and Ardyth lived up to this with their first selection, and Lucy MacNeil certainly conveys that feeling when she plays her harp. After a set of jigs on the altar, in the candlelight at the Chapel, Laoise Kelly drew a big round of applause, the audience pleasantly surprised to hear the harp played in a lively fashion.

Corrina Hewat, from north of Inverness, Scotland, was the fourth harpist on the bill. A very expressive player, she easily conveys a mood to the audience, telling a coherent story with her playing. She has a jazzy style and Stephen MacDonald remarked that "she really swings," which is clear when accompanied by pianist David Milligan. But on this night she performed solo and the jazz inflections were much more subtle, and therefore more striking, against the backdrop of three other harps.

But no sooner do I remember that than I am brought back to the Judique Community Centre, on Cape Breton's famous Route 19 along the island's west coast, where Nova Scotia's Lieutenant Governor Myra Freeman made a presentation of appreciation to fiddle teacher Stan Chapman as some of his former students—Natalie MacMaster, Wendy MacIsaac, Kendra MacGillivray, Jackie Dunn MacIsaac, and Stephanie Wills among them—were gathered for the tribute concert "Teacher's Pets." This concert reunited Chapman and his former students, with accompaniment by Dave MacIsaac on guitar and Troy MacGillivray on piano.

That show opened with a gawd-awful, deliberate screeching as Chapman's former students attempted to tune up. It was a scene from their past, a memory these women clearly enjoyed reliving. They quickly got down to business and tuned up properly before starting to play.

The community hall was filled to overflowing, a phenomenon consistent with every Celtic Colours concert that included Natalie

MacMaster. This tribute to Stan Chapman meant he may be the only person in the world who could compete with Natalie for the spotlight—the audience awed at this opportunity to see the man who taught their beloved Natalie.

In the excitement of getting the show underway, master of ceremonies Jackie Dunn MacIsaac announced that, "Flash photography was permitted" rather than "prohibited." Natalie's first number was like a lightning storm, flashes every couple of seconds. The mistake was pointed out and the emcee amended her message, but it was an amazing light show while it lasted.

The "Giant's Ceilidh" in Englishtown lived up to its namesake with sets from Inverness County's Andrea Beaton, Ian MacDougall and Mac Morin, singer-songwriter Wally MacAulay and Doug Johnson from Glace Bay and Scottish Gaelic singer Margaret Bennett. The audience was on its feet for the finale as Mac Morin jumped up to stepdance to mouth music by Margaret Bennett.

And the highlight of that same night, at "A Touch of the Irish" in Lower River Inhabitants, was the ovation-inducing finale that brought together the Irish Cape Breton fiddling of Brenda Stubbert, the Irish Newfoundland music of A Crowd of Bold Sharemen and the fiddling of Irish sisters Liz and Yvonne Kane for a rousing set that had the large crowd practically pulsating in their seats.

Ah, the Festival Club again. One night saw final performances by Lúnasa and Natalie MacMaster. Lúnasa set the tone early at the Festival Club with a staggering set of tunes and a wave goodbye before they were whisked away, heading for Holland, driven to the Halifax airport by our tireless army of volunteer drivers.

The last set of that night featured Natalie MacMaster, Wendy MacIsaac and Mairi Rankin on fiddle, Mac Morin on piano and Cheryl Smith on the drums. This was a rare scene, even for those who frequent the late-night club with its impromptu combinations of musicians.

Another night saw fiddlers Andrea Beaton, Mairi Rankin, Shelly Campbell and Lisa MacArthur get together with Wendy

MacIsaac on piano and Buddy MacDonald on guitar. By the end
of their set they were joined by Boisdale fiddler Joe Peter MacLean
and Cheryl Smith on drums, and the session spilled over into the
Green Room—spontaneous combustion!

Not only is the Festival Club often one last chance to see a
performer, it can also provide the first glimpse. As one night's
festivities were just getting underway, the sounds of A Crowd of
Bold Sharemen drifted in through the open window and I found
myself drawn across the Gaelic College campus to see them one
last time. Liz and Yvonne Kane were around so there was also the
chance to see them perform for the first time. And who knew what
else might happen once things got rolling?

You can't be everywhere.

Tom Knapp: "While I missed the Barra MacNeils in concert,
I was at the Festival Club when they blasted through several incredible sets. I didn't catch the Kane sisters in concert, but I watched
them perform together—and share a seemingly telepathic bond as
they played—at the Club. Tommy Sands, the famed Irish singer-
songwriter whom I saw several times during the week, performed
'We'll Come Back Again,' a song he wrote that day, inspired by his
experience at Celtic Colours and performed exclusively at the Club.
There were also seven Danish students, part of a larger group
visiting the festival on a government scholarship, who performed
a selection of their native folk music after a somewhat zany backstage jam.

"The only downside this year was an increased level of regi-
mentation by planners. They sacrificed some of the Club's
spontaneity and, let's face it, chaos, for organization meant to guarantee that someone was always on deck to come on stage and
perform. Unfortunately, the stricter handling of the Club led to
fewer pickup bands than we've seen in previous years. Still, the
Club remains the best place to see some of the festival's freshest
performances.

"Nor—keeping with tradition—does the excitement end when

the Club closes its doors. After-hours sessions, closed to the public, but open to a fortunate few, often continue in the Green Room till the sun comes up. Combo performances one week sprang from a magical recipe that included one-half of Newfoundland's A Crowd of Bold Sharemen, two-thirds of Ireland's Lúnasa plus Irish fiddler Liz Kane, Cape Breton fiddlers Mairi Rankin and Lisa MacArthur, and more. There was less volume—no less enthusiasm—when Natalie MacMaster slid behind the keyboard to pound out an accompaniment to a medley by fiddler Joe Peter MacLean, who also carried his banjo around that year.

"New this year were afternoon sessions in the pub above the Great Hall. Running from 1 to 5 p.m. on weekdays and led by local fiddlers Sandy MacIntyre and Dara Smith, these sessions were open to anyone who could fit into the small room to play, sing or listen—sessions being the backbone of Cape Breton's musical culture.

"One of the most amazing experiences at the club that year started after the appointed closing time. Somewhere after 3 a.m., Tim O'Brien climbed on stage with a wonderfully diverse supporting band—Mairi Rankin on fiddle, Matt Foulds on drums, Gordie Sampson on guitar, David Milligan on keyboards, Dirk Powell on bass and accordion, and Donald Hay on hand percussion. The set that followed, which ran till after 5, offered a varied menu from a distinctly non-Hendrix version of 'Hey Joe' to Cash's 'Folsum Prison Blues' and, of course some lively fiddle medleys. The dance floor was jammed and the audience, like the musicians, showed no signs of tiring as the night crept towards sunrise. As the crowd onstage expanded—adding Jeremiah McDade on soprano sax, Solon McDade on bass, François Taillefer on hand drums and Courtney Granger on fiddle—the music swung through 'Cotton-Eyed Joe,' the Gospel piece 'See What the Lord Has Done,' 'Shady Grove' and a lively Cajun set. O'Brien and Powell both switched to fiddles for a blast of Celtic tunes done bluegrass style before they finally called it a morning—and headed back to the Green Room for more."

With the coming and going of another Celtic Colours International Festival, someone remarked to me that it's "just like that feeling at Christmas. The excitement builds for weeks, and then poof, it's over." Such would certainly be the case for the hundreds of volunteers who each and every year devote nine days in October to preserving and promoting Cape Breton's culture. Many vacations are booked well in advance in order to sign on for the unending lists of tasks required to bring Celtic Colours to life.

Cape Breton veteran singer/songwriter Buddy MacDonald explains, "As a singer, I'm excited to see people like David Francey, James Keelaghan, Le Vent du Nord, and it's always nice to see some of the returnees to the festival." But he emphasizes that it's the dedication of the volunteers, along with the respectful treatment of the artists, that sets Celtic Colours apart. "Everyone loves it here, they can all relax and totally enjoy themselves, with first class treatment every year." Of course MacDonald has a secret for keeping up the pace of the festival: "Coffee, lots of coffee, with an average of three hours sleep each day. It's the only thing to keep you going!"

**Max and Joella saw the debut of The Unusual Suspects—a 32-piece orchestra of Scottish folk musicians—at the Celtic Connections festival in Glasgow, Scotland.**

It was a concept that Scottish pianist David Milligan and harp player Corrina Hewat—who both have backgrounds in jazz as well as traditional music—had been working on since the mid-1990s. Their vision comes from the idea that traditional musicians play traditional-style music and, while they don't want to change that, they might welcome the challenge of the big band format. So, in order to mix things up a bit, David and Corrina came up with the idea of giving musicians a chance to play the music they love, in the style they love, but within a big band situation—which includes a rhythm section, a horn section, tunes players, chordal tunes players and singers.

At Celtic Connections, Joella immediately talked to David and Corrina about whether or not it was feasible for this to work at Celtic Colours in Cape Breton. They said they'd like to try it out. It was agreed that, for that upcoming year, they would be the Artists in Residence along with Cape Breton's Gordie Sampson.

Over the summer, they would gather—over speaker phones, with David and Corrina in Scotland and Gordie and Joella in Cape Breton—and have static-y, hours-long conversations, discussing and exchanging tunes and working out arrangements and deciding on the line-up of players.

All the while Gordie and David and Corrina were exchanging PDFs of tunes by e-mail.

The twenty-six-piece folk orchestra would include fiddles, pipes, whistles, accordions and vocalists, complete with a seven-piece rhythm section and a four-piece horn section.

But how does a horn section fit into traditional music? And who would you even get to play horns?

Well, the leader of the pack was Rick Taylor, on trombone. He had arranged the horn parts and played in the original Unusual Suspects. Joella reports, "Corrina said, 'I don't know anything about horns. I need Rick to be there.' And then we started putting horn players around Rick. And it was very important to have Drummy (Donald Hay) and Matthew because they had two percussionists in the original and they both knew the material." Well-known Halifax-based saxophonist Jeff Goodspeed was an obvious choice. "And Rick Waychesko was Jeff's recommendation."

Obviously the Cape Breton players—from the Barra MacNeils and Beòlach to Gordie and Allie Bennett and Bruce MacPhee— had played together before and knew a bunch of the same tunes. The same with the Scottish contingent—fiddlers Sarah McFadyen and Eilidh Shaw, accordion player Inge Thomson, and singer/flute player Nuala Kennedy who played together in Harem Scarem, Rick Taylor on trombone, Martin Green on accordion, and David and Corrina's Bachue bandmate Donald Hay on percussion. And where Nova Scotia flute player Chris Norman and guitarist Andy Thurston, who play together regularly, may have had more in common musically with Nuala than, say, Martin, there was Matt Foulds on drums, who was a real connecting link, having played extensively in Cape Breton, both with Gordie and Beòlach.

On they went, mixing traditional tunes with compositions by the Artists in Residence as well as tunes by Ryan J. MacNeil, Nuala Kennedy, Martin Green, Eilidh Shaw, Chris Norman, Jerry Holland, Winston "Scotty" Fitzgerald, Dan R. MacDonald, John Morris Rankin, J. Scott Skinner and others.

"The Unusual Suspects of Celtic Colours" was scheduled for two shows, Friday in Glace Bay and Saturday in Mabou. Rehearsals only began on Tuesday, at Highland House, one of the Gaelic College residences.

Before rehearsals even began, David and Corrina and Gordie were on site, getting set up and organized for the task ahead. Declan

O'Doherty and Jennifer Currie were already there, arranging chairs and finding music stands. Before the band arrived, the music all had to be printed, copied, organized.

The table is set up in the rehearsal room behind Gordie and David and Corrina, facing the orchestra. It is actually a ping-pong table, commandeered from the artists' games room. The table is littered with neat piles of papers—scores, sheet music for various parts of the orchestra, maps of the campus—and not-so-neat piles of paper, discarded coffee cups, a couple of clipboards, half-full water bottles, someone's jacket, chord charts, a list of the tunes and what key they're played in, copies of the rehearsal CD, file folders with sticky notes all over them. Jennifer's sitting there, methodically organizing piles of paper, collating single sheets of music and putting them into folders for each section of the orchestra. Declan comes in with his arms piled full of more pages, more file folders and a smile on his face despite the tired in his eyes. He puts the papers down on the table and goes over to make some more coffee.

While most of the group takes a break, Mairi Rankin and Wendy MacIsaac go over the stepdance set with Gordie as guitarist. Andy Thurston looks on, and plays along, reading the sheet music over Gordie's shoulder. A very pregnant Lucy MacNeil is sitting watching, and Allie Bennett is still in his seat, leg pumping furiously in time to the music. Foulds, Rick Taylor, David Milligan and Donald Hay step outside for a smoke and a chat.

Corrina comes over to the table next to Jennifer, and leans over to make some notes. Jennifer hands her a pen and a piece of paper. Eilidh Shaw, coffee in hand, picks through a pile of file folders looking for her music. As they gather back into their spots, milling around their instruments and music stands, balancing coffee cups and sheets of music, a round of "Happy Birthday" breaks out dedicated to Sheumas MacNeil—with a big drum bit at the end, Gordie on the kit, David playing shaker and Matt on congas. Sax, accordion, and flute join in. Jamie Gatti has his shades on, and everybody's smiling.

Rehearsals started in the morning, which is not something to look forward to when you have the Festival Club also occupying some of the space known as morning. But rehearse they did, day after day, as the week wore on, despite whatever suffering they may have set themselves up for the night before.

"It was hard for them," admits Joella, "'cause we did need to use some of them for shows in the evenings. So, three, four o'clock, people would need to leave to go to soundcheck. You just can't afford to do this at a festival and not use them for other things. So they were all exhausted but exhilarated the whole time."

With everybody present and accounted for, more or less, David, Gordie and Corrina get back to work, sitting at the front of the room, facing the orchestra-to-be—Gordie with guitar in hand behind a music stand, David and Corrina on either side of him at piano and harp. Everyone is reading from charts, some relying on them more than others. Rehearsing the accordion feature, David stands at the piano giving notes at the end of a run-through. "On the third time through, you just go, 'Bedi'didi'didi'dadi dadi,'" he says helpfully, he hopes, miming the timing with his fingers on bass, air-guitar style, "and that'll put everything on the beat." Semi-confused murmuring prompts him to play it once on the piano to illustrate his point, and they run through it one more time.

"It was good though because we were working till like eleven each night, more or less, ten or eleven o'clock," says David. "And there was that kind of dead period between when people kinda got back from gigs and the Festival Club hadn't quite kicked off. And it was like, well, we might as well just use the time, so that was when all the writing and printing and copying got done. It was quite a good system actually. And it was probably quite good that we didn't have anything, you know that there wasn't a bar open or there was nobody else around so it was like—okay, let's just get on with it. And then when the Festival Club did start, we could just go and party."

One of the tunes—"Hull's Reel"—wasn't coming together and drove a couple of folks into Baddeck to the Yellow Cello to eat and get off campus for a while. Somebody sang the tune—it could have been Corrina or David or Wendy or Mairi—then everybody had a go at jigging the tune the way they play it. And as everybody ended up singing it together, somebody suggested that they do that in the gig. It was agreed, let's just sing it.

"A lot of people just kind of hung out together that wouldn't necessarily have done that if we'd just been at the festival doing separate things," says David, noting that there were a few special moments starting to happen in the Festival Club as well. Like when the horn section suddenly appeared on stage one night mid-week, just sitting in with everybody, working on their chops, figuring out how to play together for the big gig.

"You can't beat sort of sitting across from somebody for a week and sharing tunes and learning their tunes and they're learning your tunes. I mean there's nothing like it. And then the overwhelming sound, when you either work as a small band or duos or solos or whatever, to all of sudden have this huge, full orchestral sound—it's amazing. It's a wonderful experience for the artists. I mean, I still say it's one of the best things we ever did."

"Partied hard. Rehearsed hard," says Corrina.

And then it was showtime.

The Unusual Suspects concert opens with the familiar "Lord Lovat's Lament" played by Corrina on the harp, accompanied by piano, guitar and percussion. And then the fiddles kick in with an Angus R. Beaton tune, and spurred on by the pipes and the horns, a couple of traditional numbers and one each by J. Scott Skinner and Jerry Holland as the flutes and whistles are introduced, trading off the melody with the fiddles as the big band builds up to a suitably big finish with the pipes and horns leading the way, a couple of syncopated stops, and a final run with the most tasteful horn hits, finished by the fiddles—and the show is on its way.

"How're you guys doing?" Gordie asks the audience as he introduces the "Silly Wizard" song written by Andy M. Stewart, sometimes known as "Strathlorne" in Cape Breton. It's a nice gentle arrangement with contributions from everyone scattered throughout, including a smooth bass solo by Jamie Gatti and Corrina's harmonies with Gordie.

The flutes and whistles are introduced now: Ryan MacNeil, Bruce MacPhee, Nuala Kennedy and Chris Norman. They start with a tune by Chris, Chris's playing accompanied by bowed bass and then harp. Nuala Kennedy's flute joins in as they transition into "Blair Dwight Brown," written by Nuala for Transportation Coordinator Blair Brown. Ryan picks up the tempo on flute with his own "Reel for Spanky." The horns help transition into a tune on the highland pipes played by Bruce and then start hitting the off beats as the fiddles take up the lead. And around it goes again to another dramatic ending.

And the audience is really getting a taste for this.

"If you're counting your Barra MacNeils on stage, you'll notice that one is missing," says David, welcoming Sheumas.

"Well I'm one Barra MacNeil who's hard to miss," says a very pregnant Lucy, standing behind a microphone with Stewart, getting ready to sing the Gaelic song "The Apple Tree"—and everyone gets in on the somewhat jazzy arrangement.

The accordions are up next—Stewart MacNeil, Inge Thomson and Martin Green. It's interesting to hear how the three accordions work together, weaving in and out of what each other is doing, bass lines carrying on through into the next tune, picking up the tempo ever so slightly. Wendy and Allie are in the fiddle section in front of them, swaying and bobbing, fiddles in hand, dancing in their seats as the next tune comes around and the percussion picks it up. And then the fiddles are back under their chins. The horns add a touch here and there before the accordions take over again. Allie turns his head over his shoulder to look back at the accordions with a smile on his face.

Mairi Rankin and Wendy MacIsaac come centre stage, dressed in black. They dance in unison, arms by their sides as Gordie picks out the tune. The crowd cheers them on as the tune picks up. And in come the fiddles.

Then Corrina is joined by Gordie, Lucy, Stewart, Sheumas, Nuala and Inge for the Scottish song "The Cruel Sister." They exchange leads and intertwining harmonies. It's a long and mournful song, but fully engaging in this arrangement. The voices blend beautifully.

The first set closes with another set of tunes. More of the same: sparkling, unexpected arrangements, building up through the sections until everyone on stage is playing. They take our breath away with the sheer power of the sound of this folk orchestra.

And the first half ends with a standing ovation.

Sam MacPhee, from the Gaelic College in St. Ann's, does the draw—to Andrea Turner from Santa Rosa, California—an autographed poster and compilation CD. And then the obligatory "left your lights on" announcement.

"Also there was a ring found in the women's washroom if anyone's lost a ring," announced the emcee.

"Or a wife," someone yells from the crowd, to great applause.

Seated at her harp, Corrina thanks the audience for coming back. And then thanks the band for coming back, to applause and a few laughs. She introduces a piece commissioned for the festival that she and David and Gordie wrote.

It's very orchestral, thoughtful. Then the accordions pick up a tune and then the others, until it breaks down to a drum beat and Jeff Goodspeed steps up on sax, and they take turns. And then before you know it the pipes are back. And then they exchange with the horns. And the horns rock it to the end.

# When I was first hired as Information Officer for Celtic Colours, it was after two years of volunteering as a driver.

Driving was a hectic and exhilarating blur of an experience—meeting people, driving around the island, seeing so much new music and dealing with the logistics. In many ways the drivers are the face of the festival. And, it's a great way to see how the festival works. But once I took the job and moved in to the office I really got to see that putting on this festival is a big job. Max MacDonald and Joella Foulds, as Festival Directors, were at it all year long, along with Office Manager Marg LeBlanc; others come in on contract or term positions. My job as Information Officer typically started in June and ran until the end of October.

The Charlotte Street office was grimy but nice. Shauna was there, and Nigel Kearns, and we had a good time working together through the summer, in the stuffy little office, figuring it out as we went along. It was kind of like a mix between summer camp and summer school. We'd work late and sneak in a few beers if it was hot out. And finish up and go out to see someone play around town. Shauna and Max and Marg would be working late, smoking their brains out because you could smoke back then, although it was starting to border on impolite, especially for the non-smoking Joella. But she never did complain.

It is two-thirds through June, the first day of summer. I've been back to work for three full weeks now. I'm into my fourth week and by the end of this week I have to have all the information about this year's festival ready to be released to the public. This year there are forty-eight concerts scheduled for nine days in October and still a few of the shows aren't fully put together; some don't have names yet. Max is working on show descriptions for the website and program. Joella is dealing with artists and managers, programming the concerts, and putting the final touches on the line-ups.

"This one needs a local fiddler . . . . That one needs an international presence . . . . Won't it be great to see these folks play in the same concert and imagine the encore when they all get together at the end?"

"Oh, we need some singing in that show . . . . And didn't he play in that concert last year?"

"What're we gonna call this show?

Concerts are themed and named. How else are you going to keep track of forty-plus shows, four and five a day, featuring at least three acts each? You name them. "The Whycocomagh Gathering," "Louisbourg Crossroads," "Raising the Roof," "Tunes for the Mira." Some names are obvious, others take a lot of work and a liberal dose of lateral thinking. And it's a team sport in the office. While the bulk of shows are named from conception or by acclamation or tradition, there are always a tricky few that stay tantalizingly out of reach. When it gets to that point, everyone in the office is wandering into our space from time to time and looking at The Board and sort of mumbling to themselves. Occasionally there's a Eureka! moment and a big deal is made all around about getting one more name up on the board before it's time to start releasing the information to the public.

And how do you organize hundreds of artists into a series of concerts that will appeal to the ticket-buying public and the hardcore Celtic music enthusiasts? You tie each show together with a theme, relating to the location, the featured act, the combination of performers or some event. "Celtic Women" in Port Hawkesbury showcased talented women performers from all over the Celtic world. In 2010 "Celtic Women" became "Women in Tune" so as not to cause confusion with the "Celtic Women: Songs from the Heart" phenomenon. "Close to the Floor" in Judique recognized the connection between Cape Breton's traditional music and Cape Breton's dance tradition. "Dangerous Duos" at the Savoy paired a versatile handful of local players and singers with many and varied visiting artists from Scotland, Ireland and the United States. "The Beatons of Mabou," "The MacLellan Trio Reunion," "Lee's Legacy," "Bards and Ballads," "Celtic Pianos," "Whelan Meets Winnie"—and so on.

The schedule/line-up changes several times a day this time of year, but I only update my files once a day. This much I have learned: it is too easy to miss a midday alteration that may happen while you are on the phone, out to lunch, or in the bathroom. There was a time when I'd try to make updates as they happened, every time Joella got off the phone and came into the office to change a name and a date or a concert or an accompanist. Each change required me to go through a collection of Word documents and Excel spreadsheets that listed artists and bios, show schedules, show descriptions, show line-ups, and various combinations including elements of all these other documents along with details like prices and times and venues and communities. I track down the info in a couple of documents, make the changes, and print the updated versions, pass them around the office and ask for the copies of the old ones back, so there's no confusion—hopefully. Inevitably, something would get missed and as soon as the information was released to the public through the press and to the website in a week or so, someone would notice their name missing from a line-up. And I'd get a call or an e-mail or, most often, Joella would bring it to my attention because she got the call or e-mail. And I'd look up to the board and see it there, plain as day, and wonder why I never noticed it before. In an undertaking such as this—a nine-day festival staged all over Cape Breton featuring hundreds of artists from half a dozen countries—it's the details that really make it happen. And it's the Production Coordinator's job to take care of a lot of those details.

Thankfully this madness was greatly reduced with the introduction of *Marcato Festival* management software, which was developed in Cape Breton with Celtic Colours as a test case. The custom-tailored database software has greatly improved the organization and accuracy of information used by festival staff and volunteers as well as what gets presented to the general public through the website.

But until Marcato came along, organization of all this information fell to the Production Coordinator and the systems put in place by Shauna Walters who has worked with Celtic Colours in various roles (Production Coordinator, Transportation Coordinator, Festival Club Manager, Presenters and Media Program, and Site and Stage Manager) over the years. In the early years of the festival, Shauna was instrumental in working out the nitty gritty logistics, while Max and Joella worked on the actual programming. "I was the database," she says now.

This is the time of year, June, when things really start to happen in the office. The space I occupy is shared with a Production Coordinator who makes all the arrangements for artists from traveling and accommodations to meals, itineraries, contracts and tax waivers for international artists. This person is responsible for making sure the artists have a hassle-free experience at Celtic Colours, that they get here and get back home, that they have somewhere to stay and something to eat, that their contracts are in order and that they get paid. This is the person who tries to make sure that the artists are happy because happy artists tell others about what a wonderful time they had at Celtic Colours International Festival on Cape Breton Island. And good word of mouth is publicity you cannot buy for any price.

By the time the Production Coordinator starts work, I've already been there a month. This office that we share—usually with a Technical Coordinator who oversees all aspects of sound reinforcement, lighting and the logistics of having six or seven production crews running all over Cape Breton Island for a week and a half—is where the festival starts to take shape in a real way. Max has his office where he deals with marketing and promotion, and Joella has her office where she deals mainly with artistic aspects, designing the concerts, dealing with the artists and/or management, as well as coordinating the community workshops and the schools program.

And they meet in the middle, in my office, to look at The Board.

The Board is a wall-sized piece of sheet metal, painted white, with nine columns drawn on it that correspond to the nine days of the Celtic Colours Festival. Pieces of fridge magnet, cut into one-inch-by-four-inch rectangles, are labeled with artists' names and with the communities where the concerts will be held. And this is where the concerts start to take shape. The Board shows us what is happening day-by-day, who is playing where and when and with whom.

For the first month, this is my life. Watching the schedule adjusted daily, as artist availability changes or new combinations of performers reveal themselves. And then one day, everything else changes. Tickets go on sale in mid-July and no fewer than two weeks before that date we must have all the information—who is who; when and where are they playing; what are the shows called; who is playing with whom; what are the ticket prices; where are the venues; how do you get there; where do you get tickets—available to the public so they can make decisions for which concerts they want to buy tickets.

Next thing is to get the website in order. I work closely with Ralph Dillon, who is the web-master—he gets all the information online. Weldon Bona of Absolute Design told me that when the leaves start to come out, it's time for him to start working on the festival. For Ralph and me, the Celtic Colour in the leaves is green. And we don't rest until they're all on the ground!

Bona is responsible for the "look" of the festival. He designs the posters—one for the festival itself and one for each show—which are distributed to the community hosting organizations—and the print advertising which is placed in local and regional daily and weekly newspapers and magazines all over the world. Our ongoing major challenge is to produce the Official Program.

The Program is meant to be a one-stop place for festival information. We start with show descriptions, a one-glance schedule, artist bios, a welcome from the board, politicians and festival directors, along with photos of the artists and a description for every show. As Weldon develops the look of the program, I am searching for artists' photos, writing, re-writing, editing and proofing artist bios and show descriptions and proofreading the schedule for accuracy. Show descriptions are group efforts between Max, Joella and me. They tend to draft descriptions to convey their vision of each show and then I'll edit to the space. Some of the bios are submitted and need only to be edited down. Others have to be updated, rewritten or written from scratch. Typically I write up the local players, while the national and international artists will need updates and editing. Photos are another story. We usually come up with a mix of submitted press shots and action shots from the festival archives and various other local sources.

August is madness. It's just getting hot out usually sometime late in July. And sometimes it gets unbearably hot. My office is the only one with an air conditioner, and while I resisted its simple installation early on, preferring the nice fresh-not-frigid air through an open window, I came around to enjoy its comfort as much as everyone else in the office—who suddenly have many reasons to visit my little space.

Those reasons aren't just to enjoy the cool, conditioned air. The Production Coordinator and Technical Coordinator or Volunteer Coordinator have moved in by now, and the traffic in and out of the small office space increases noticeably. This is the time of year when things really start to get rolling. The board has pretty much stopped changing and the line-up is being absorbed by osmosis from looking at it and living with it for a couple of months. The show names are well known internally and the schedule widely publicized outside the room. Tickets are selling, shows are selling out, phone calls are coming in requesting information about the festival and the island and the individual show posters have been delivered to the hosting communities.

Media interest has had a little spike from the press release announcing the line-up toward the end of June and the proofreaders have started calling from editorial offices in London, New York and Los Angeles to check on their freelancers' stories. Others request photos for travel pieces that mention the festival—local daily papers and international monthly magazines for publication in California and Ireland and Germany and Russia and around the world. Ralph has the website up to date and attracting visitors worldwide, and e-mails from first-timers and old friends of the festival start to pour in. Preparation has begun for the official program, and planning for the international export and trade program is underway, provided funding has been secured to invest in this important aspect of the festival. By now, I have had about one sleepless night for each of these aspects of the festival. Celtic Colours is about two months away and it's summer in Cape Breton.

Summer in Cape Breton is just about the busiest time of the year. There's a community festival or celebration just about every weekend and people are everywhere—folks who have been working away for months or years; tourists here for the first time; random visitors in for a wedding or entertainment event; and the residents such festivities bring out of the woodwork. The weather is pleasant, generally, especially compared to the dreariness of a long cold winter. It's a tough time of the year to be so busy with work. But that's what it's all about, really, attracting a big crowd of people from home and away for a major entertainment event. The festival is nine days of music, just about around the clock, and if you're working on an event like this, you've got to be sure you're ready for it. You can't find out in the middle of the week after Thanksgiving that you just can't stay up till all hours of the night and function the next day and for the next couple of days. So I try to take advantage of the busiest time of the year by taking in some of the events and festivities, checking on my stamina and guts—training, if you will, to make sure I'm up to the festival's October challenge. Better to find out I can't make it through the next day at work in the summer than during the festival itself.

Because the festival itself is always a blur. Weeks before it starts everything goes into fast forward. Suddenly it's everything at once. You can plan for it, but you need fractals to cover all the possible combinations of what could happen. What could go right as well as what could go wrong. You just never know how it's gonna float until you put it in the water. But it's an exciting time, seeing where the holes are and getting them plugged up enough to bail water until you can get 'er on an even keel.

The weeks before the festival disintegrate into chaos, not quite full-blown chaos because the festival itself isn't actually happening yet. The real chaos comes later. But there are the first signs of it. The week or two before the festival actually starts turn into what seems like about three days—three very long days. It's hard to say where the time goes. I have literally sat down in the morning and opened a file that I needed to work on and not seen that file again until I close it at night before I head home, barely having had a chance to eat, so burnt out from the constant demands of the day.

It's crazy. Four telephone lines ringing and everybody in the room already has a phone to the ear. There's a constant demand on your time. You answer the phone while you are doing whatever else it is that you need to get done—while the Production Coordinator is finalizing an international artist's travel arrangements, festival itinerary and government paperwork, and the Volunteer Coordinator is organizing hundreds of volunteers in a dozen different capacities from communities all over the island, and the Information Officer is writing a press release and proofing an ad for the next day's newspaper—and the phone rings. And somebody jumps on it. Julia Knowles, the Volunteer Coordinator, is checking notes between making calls, mostly to leave messages since no one is home. She almost absently reaches out and nabs it. "Celtic Colours . . . ." I hardly even notice the phone ring. I'm proofreading ads and I recognize at a glance that I have proofed these before for another publication. I know exactly what should be changed and only have to make sure there are no typos or information missing. And I know just where to look. That'll save some time, not having to read the whole thing. The press release on the other hand needs something. Not much, just a little something. And that's going to take time.

"Do you have a schedule of workshops for international artists?"

asks Production Coordinator Dianne MacPhee, impatient because she knows she should have had this information long ago, and she did have it, but thought that it might have been changed, not been updated.

"Should be on the website," I answer over my shoulder, wondering now if it had been updated on the website yet. Wondering if that was on my list before sending out the press release, which was still being written, or if I still had to confirm some of that information which, it had been decided, would have to wait until after proofing this ad, and I was still waiting on confirmation of something. The ad had come in just on deadline and had to be turned around right away. The website update wasn't as urgent, though it still needed to be done next. And it would still have to wait until the press release was ready to go out.

"It's not there," confirms Dianne as I start looking for the information update. I realize it could be in any of these e-mails from half a dozen people. I'm going through recent files, new e-mails and available pieces of paper scribbled with notes and telephone messages scattered all over my desk.

The workshop schedule can be particularly chaotic. Workshops are organized by the community group that is hosting the event. Yvette Rogers has been dealing with this since becoming Outreach Coordinator. There is no set timetable for when details need to be finalized, and while every effort is made to get these details nailed down early, things change and plans need to be adjusted. Volunteer groups, non-profit organizations, and professional institutions alike face these challenges, but it's a big job to coordinate a full day or two or three, or even a week, of activities. Hundreds, over the years. Keeping track of all the changes in each of their schedules, and ensuring the proper people get updated on the changes—the general public who phone and ask or get the information from the website; the Transportation Coordinator when there is a festival artist involved, unless it's local artists who usually provide their own transportation, unless they are staying at the College in which case they usually don't; and now the Production Coordinator needs to know for the itinerary she is trying to complete. And now the Information Officer has to find that information.

The phone rings again. Julia is already on the phone, having just reached a potential volunteer she has been trying to contact for days, someone who may be able to fill a key role in her operations. I'm hunched down over my keyboard defiantly ignoring the interruption so I can search for the missing information. "Must find this information," I say with my shoulders, shuddering through the second ring, knowing that Dianne is held up in finishing her itinerary until I confirm this stuff for her. "Celtic Colours," she almost growls in frustration, thinking, Will I ever get this finished so I can go on to what I need to get done today in order for things to work tomorrow? The festival is only a week away—not even a week away, she realizes in a panic. And these itineraries needed to be in the mail this morning in order to get there on time. And the information keeps changing. And this person on the phone has never been to the festival before and is wondering which shows have fiddle music in them. "Actually, we have dozens of shows with fiddle music during those nine days and they're scattered all over the island. On Friday, there's a show in . . . ."

Good, thinks Dave—who couldn't help but hear her end of the conversation as they sat only the width of a desk apart. He's had that call before. It can be a long one, explaining the logistics of a festival like this to someone who is only vaguely familiar with where in the world is Cape Breton Island. "That should give me time to see if that updated workshop information has come in yet," he mumbles to himself. And to make a call if it hasn't. But wait, that's it. That's what the press release needs. Something about the workshops. And if this international artist is confirmed for that workshop, that will tie it all together. The phone rings again. "And then I can use that quote about how the international artists from the festival really get involved at the local level." Dave's talking to himself just a little louder than under his breath, tuning out the ring as he looks through a previous draft for that quote he knows is there somewhere, excited by the possibility of getting the press release ready to be proofed and out by the end of the day. And off his desk. Second ring and he overhears Dianne explaining on her end of the phone that there is no pass for the whole week because the ticket prices vary and there are actually as many as five or six shows in a single day. She looks at Dave smugly, with a "Sorry I'm tied up on this call" kind of look.

"Well that sounds great," says Julia, quickly jotting down a few notes as she hangs up, silencing the third ring in the same motion. "Celtic Colours . . . ."

Dodged another one, thinks Dave, bouncing a hurt look back at Dianne, as if he can't believe she wouldn't drop everything to help him out of a jam, and a "Thanks Julia" look in her direction. Now to find that quote. No, need to confirm the information first. Julia's voice interrupts that thought.

"Can I tell him who's calling?" She puts the call on hold. "It's about the ad proof," she says, "can you take it?"

"Just tell him it'll be there in twenty minutes," says Dave as he shuffles through the papers on his desk to bring the ad proof back to the top of the pile, taking a quick glance at it and starting to reply to the e-mail requesting the ad proof. Just a few changes, he notices, better just take care of this now, there's not much to it. The phone rings yet again. And Julia is on another call already, introducing herself to another potential volunteer. Dianne is also still on her call, now patiently explaining that this is the Festival Office and to book tickets you have to call the Box Office. Second ring and she's explaining that there are airports in Halifax and Sydney, and that Sydney is on Cape Breton Island and Halifax is about five hours away on the mainland.

One more thing to check on the ad proof . . . . Third ring . . . . Nobody else makes a move for it, both tied up in conversation. He's so close to actually getting to work on his work, but ringing phones must be answered. He hopes he can hold that thought. "Celtic Colours International Festival. Dave speaking . . . ."

"Hi. I'm calling from Santa Monica and I just heard about this Celtic Colours festival?" Celtic pronounced with the soft "s" sound, like basketball's Boston Celtics. "And I was looking for some more information. Thinking about coming up there to Nova Scotia, for the first time. Always wanted to make it out to that part of your country. We've heard it's just absolutely beautiful and this looks like a good time to do it. We just retired, you know, and I think it will make a great anniversary gift for my husband. So, tell me about the festival. When does the festival start?"

And the media carry Celtic Colours to the wider world. Some of the more than eight dozen individuals and media outlets covering Celtic Colours in one year included: *Irish Music Magazine* (Ireland); *Performing Songwriter Magazine* (Tennessee); *The Sunday Herald* (Scotland); *The Independent* (Scotland); *The Scotsman* (Scotland); *Irish Echo* (New York); *Pathfinders' Travel Magazine* (Pennsylvania); *Profile Magazine* (New York); *The Shetland Post* (Shetland); *The Gazette* (Montreal); ATV *Live at Five*; CBC Radio One (*Atlantic Airwaves*); BBC Radio Scotland; BBC Radio Nan Gaidheal; WERU FM (Maine); KTAOS FM (New Mexico, Solar Radio); CIGO FM (Port Hawkesbury); CJFX (Antigonish); and CKJM (Chéticamp).

Glenn Meisner and CBC Radio's *Atlantic Airwaves* have recorded Celtic Colours since the beginning, and then broadcast those concerts during the summer and winter. Using the festival as a backdrop, they also produced a two-hour special, with David Francey as the host, exploring the music and culture of Cape Breton.

Throughout the year Wendy Bergfelt of *Mainstreet* and *Island Echoes* and the staff of *Information Morning*—all CBC Sydney— broadcast concerts and interviews dealing with Celtic Colours.

One year CBC TV's *The National* hosted by Ross Porter, wanted a profile of Natalie MacMaster. They piled into a couple of the smallest venues in the festival, following Natalie around. Of course, the shows were sold out to the rafters. And a TV crew, even a small one, isn't likely to include fewer than four people. And TV crews can be demanding and are prone to get in the way. On this particular night in Glendale, the CBC suppertime news show was broadcasting live from the hall, Glenn Meisner and Pat Martin had their truck set up outside to tape the show for CBC Radio's Atlantic Airwaves and the TV crew was there to tape the show for the television special. The venue was so packed, the only way to cross the room was to go outside and come back in the door nearest where you wanted to get.

As word spreads about Celtic Colours and it is known to be not a one-off but a year-after-year pretty spectacular event, Youtube samples and blog comments find their way to the internet airways. I won't even try to suggest what to look for on Youtube—you just put in the name of most artists who have played Celtic Colours and something interesting comes up. But for a terrific example of cross-generation performance, try this one: http://www.youtube.com/watch?v=KTDyNQY0A8Y. It's Ashley MacIsaac with Buddy MacMaster, opening for the White Stripes at the Savoy Theatre in Glace Bay. It is not Celtic Colours. It's certainly the spirit. Consider it a bonus track.

And the bloggers are out there as well. Victor Maurice Faubert from New Jersey writes an internet blog describing both music and dance from many years of the Celtic Colours festival, as well as some enticing hikes through the Cape Breton landscape. Here's a taste:

Friday, I got in a pretty good hike up Fair Alastair and back to the trail head via MacKinnons Brook Lane. The sun was hiding much of the time, but it lit up the gorgeous landscape in interesting ways from moment to moment; it finally came out on the way back and, together with the singing brook, gorged from recent rain, put me in a sunny mood for the official opening concert of Celtic Colours at Port Hawkesbury. There was also a duplicate official opening concert at Sydney with different performers. This was a very fine show. Jeff MacDonald's Gaelic singing was an enjoyable opening, and his and Brian Ó'hEadhra's later rendition of the beautiful "Tàladh na Beinne Guirme" (The Big Mountain's Lullaby), which they co-wrote, was stunning. For me, the best of a very fine evening was Jerry Holland and Marion Dewar, a powerhouse duo of Scottish traditional music not to be missed! Sabra MacGillivray's dancing to Jerry and Marion's music was well received. Phil

Cunningham (accordion), Duncan Chisholm (fiddle), and Kris Drever (guitar) did some very fine sets and the MacQuarrie Dancers, in another highlight of the evening for me, performed a choreographed piece to Phil's "The Colours of Cape Breton," a beautiful slow air he wrote while attending a previous Celtic Colours. I had not previously known of Duncan Chisholm nor of Kris Drever, both from Northern Scotland; Duncan is a tremendously gifted fiddler and Kris is an equally talented guitar player. Joe Derrane and the Boston Edge brought a taste of well-played Irish-American music. And the Blazin' Fiddles certainly lived up to their name, even though one of their number was still in Scotland where his wife was giving birth; what an amazing, energetic group and what blazing tempos!

Saturday morning, Candy Cooke inveigled me into attending a Gaelic singing workshop at the Mabou Féis conducted by Cookie and Heather Rankin. Intended for children, we were welcomed into the group, but of course there was no question of my actually singing—my voice is worse than a crow's. What a privilege it was to hear the Rankins' wonderful voices raised in song and, having once been a high-school teacher, to observe their masterful command of teaching techniques guaranteed to grab and hold the attention of the roughly fifteen youngsters ranging in age from maybe four to ten, getting them to learn the Gaelic song "Mo Rùn Geal Dìleas." And learn it they did, giving a rousing rendition before the hour was out.

Saturday afternoon, I attended the concert at St. Matthew's United Church in Inverness, dedicated to "tune-makers" and featuring the prolific Cape Breton composers Kinnon Beaton, Jerry Holland, and Brenda Stubbert, along with Dougie MacDonald and Ryan J. MacNeil and Scotland's Phil Cunningham (accompanied by Duncan Chisholm and Kris Drever); Betty Lou Beaton, Marion Dewar, and Mac Morin provided the piano accompaniments. Each of the composers played sets of tunes they had written, most of them now an integral part of the standard repertoire wherever Cape Breton music is played. It brought home once again that Cape Breton music is not a static remembrance of the past, but a dynamic celebration of a culture that is alive and thriving, to which each generation contributes. As one can imagine, with the music being played by its composers, it was beautifully and joyfully rendered.

For the past two years, I attended the New Waterford concert on Saturday night, and debated long and hard this year whether to do so again. It's a tight drive from Inverness to New Waterford when one has less than two and one half hours. So this year, the three headliners at the Whycocomagh concert tipped me to instead attend the concert in Whycocomagh's Education Centre, which featured: David Francey, singer, story teller, and song writer; multitalented Troy, Kendra, and Sabra MacGillivray; and Le Vent du Nord, a Québécois band. The connection of David Francey to Celtic music escapes me, as does that of Le Vent du Nord (though an occasional Celtic tune could be heard in their music). Nevertheless, I really enjoyed this concert. I've heard David Francey often on WKSU's Folk Music Show on the Internet and found his performance sincere and convincing, with his stories greatly enriching the songs. The MacGillivrays, as always, put on a fantastic performance, with Sabra taking over the keyboards for the first time in public, freeing Troy to join Kendra in a fiddle duet. They are wonderfully talented siblings and the audience roared with delight at their tunes and their steps. Le Vent du Nord has to be seen to be believed; it is an amazingly energetic group—one could even say athletic group, given the continuous dancing that accompanies their music and their songs (all in French) . . . I've never encountered a warmer North Wind and those present were obviously as enchanted as I was. Towards the end of the show, they got much of the audience line dancing across the front and around the sides of the packed auditorium and had some enthusiastic volunteers join them stepdancing on the stage. The finale brought the three acts together and the dancing continued throughout.

Burton MacIntyre, the concert's host, and Myra Freeman, the Lieutenant Governor of Nova Scotia, took the stage to do some steps; I was greatly impressed that the Lieutenant Governor, who is not a native Cape Bretoner, was sufficiently interested in the Celtic culture as to have taken the time to learn how to stepdance . . . After the concert, I drove to West Mabou for the regular Saturday square dance, the only one along the Cèilidh Trail that continues throughout the entire year.

Dealing with the media is a job in itself. Media from all over the world apply for accreditation at the festival. Each form requires its own special attention.

Print journalists are generally the easiest to get along with. You supply them with background information, arrange access to the musicians and whomever else they want to interview—festival organizers, board, etc.—and you hope they approach their job professionally.

Photographers can be a little more difficult, depending on their level of professionalism. There is a strict no-flash policy. You don't want the media to interrupt the show or interfere with the ticket-buying audience's experience. A flashing photographer can do this.

And a photographer who stands in front of the audience to get a photo can do this. But it's usually the audience you have to worry about, even though there are signs at every venue prohibiting photos and recording of any kind, except by authorized personnel.

Times have changed a lot in terms of technology and, with that, my responsibilities. Now the audience can record a show on their phones and have it on Youtube before the set is over. On the one hand, by doing this, they have violated copyright laws, posting these videos without the artists' permission. This also compromises the festival because we want to protect artists from being exploited in any way while they are our guests. On the other hand, a viral video is an effective tool in new media marketing, and it can work for the artist and the festival. It's a dilemma, and means we need a serious re-think about our taping/recording/photography policy.

Dealing with radio has always been fairly non-eventful. They are usually looking for interviews with the artists. Public and community radio stations from across the United States regularly cover the festival. They are attracted by the big names, but are also interested in Cape Breton musicians. They go home to Maine or California or New Mexico with a bagful of new music to play on their Celtic specialty programs. And that's another way Cape Breton gets heard around the world.

Often journalists get the story wrong. On the other hand, I have spent hours on the phone with fact checkers from *The New York Times*, *Lexus* magazine (distributed to Lexus car-owners) and *Home and Away* (distributed to AAA members). The amount of detail they are looking for is inspiring in a day when too many media outlets don't give a damn about typos and inaccuracies.

"So my writer says he left the concert at Mabou, turned right, drove for about ten minutes on the highway, then turned onto an unlit, dirt road, drove another fifteen or twenty minutes further into the darkness and came to a little hall with a parking lot full of cars and people standing around. Inside Natalie MacMaster was playing fiddle with someone on the piano and everyone in the overflowing hall was dancing. Does that seem likely to you?"

I followed that fact checker's directions on the map while he talked, and decided that his writer must have ended up at a dance in Glencoe Mills and assured the fact checker that this was entirely plausible. I was impressed that the publication was so concerned about the details, despite the fact that it was unlikely anyone from the area would read the article and notice any inaccuracy. From our conversation, I got the feeling the fact checker was as concerned about whether the writer turned left or right as he was unsure that a big star like Natalie MacMaster would be playing a dance in a tiny hall just this side of "the middle of nowhere."

Most times, you know exactly where everyone in the media is planning to be and what they need, and everything goes smoothly. Then there are days when my cell phone rings constantly with last-minute media requests. I try to meet everyone who applies for Media Accreditation, but it's not always possible, especially if they arrive at a concert before checking in with the Media Office. One such day, I had planned to be in Louisbourg at the Playhouse to meet a film crew from a German television station whose point of introduction to the festival would be the concert that night. I had received the accreditation application, sent in by a third party who was arranging everything, and approved it. But film and television crews can be demanding and I have found that it is best if I am on hand, to let the event staff concentrate on what they need to do and for me to take care of any needs or concerns the media may have and to personally lay down the ground rules—use existing lighting, don't interfere with the concert, don't obstruct the view of the paying customers, and above all, stay off the stage.

So on this day my mission was to meet this crew in Louisbourg, which is approximately an hour and half drive away from head-quarters at the Gaelic College. Showtime is 7:30 p.m., but I planned to be there earlier to meet the crew before things got too hectic. Through the day, I got two calls that would mess with my carefully constructed plans. One was from a regional television show broad-casting from the Sydney waterfront. They wanted to talk to someone live, on air, about the festival. Max and Joella, the logical choices, were already committed so the job fell to me, with their blessing. That was fine by me. I know the host of the show, she is from Cape Breton, literally around the corner from where I grew up, and I hadn't seen her in a while. I revised my day to fit this in and decided I'd better shave my scruffy festival face if I was to be on television that evening representing the festival. While in the process of trying to scrape off and scrub away nearly a week of sleepless nights and hectic days, my phone rang again.

"Hey Dave. Max here," Max MacDonald's voice crackled over the line, sounding oddly like it was coming in both ears at once. It turned out that Max was calling from the other room, just outside the bathroom, and I could in fact hear his voice in both ears. "We just found out that the Premier is going to be at the concert in North Sydney tonight and that ATV and CBC are sending reporters to cover it. Can you drop in there and make sure everything's cool?" CBC and ATV television reporters are used to swooping in on the scene, getting their stories and getting back to the station in time to make their broadcast. That's the nature of what they do and they are accustomed to doing it their way. And their way doesn't always jibe with the way we run this festival.

"No worries," I said. "I'm on it." As I hung up my phone, I realized that now I had to be in three places, a good hour and a half drive apart from each other, at approximately the same time. And that meant I had to leave now.

So I finished shaving, found an appropriately black button-down shirt for my television interview, grabbed a couple of CDs—Rolling Stones' *Exile on Mainstreet*, a Steve Earle CD that featured a collaboration with Sharon Shannon and some soundtrack music he'd done, and AC/DC's *Back in Black*—jumped into my rented red convertible Media-mobile, and headed down the winding road from the Gaelic College towards Matthew Wesley United Church in North Sydney.

Made it in time for the *Live at 5* interview with Marianna in Sydney. Waited for the Germans in Louisbourg, but they never did show up.

**For me, Celtic Colours is Scottish piper Fred Morrison on a national broadcast of CBC's *Mainstreet* from the Savoy Theatre on Thanksgiving Day.**

Fred made a great point about not being in Cape Breton to find his roots but to explore a somewhat familiar land. "It's like visiting cousins," he said, adding that he was quite happy with his roots at home, thank you very much.

Celtic Colours is a delicious meal prepared by people who really care in a part of Cape Breton I'd never see, except for the music.

It's that time I ran into Rick Taylor in Glasgow, Scotland. We spotted each other in the lobby of the Holiday Inn and met up beside the bar. I told him I had a copy of CBC's recording of the "Unusual Suspects of Celtic Colours" from 2004. Rick was excited to hear it and after making sure I was properly taken care of in this foreign land—he was eager to return the hospitality he enjoyed so much in Cape Breton—we went directly to his room and listened to the recording, laughing and drinking and telling stories appreciatively throughout. Later that week I heard a hotel manager had to come up to the floor Rick's room was on, in response to a noise complaint. When he found Rick and several others in the hallway singing, the manager demanded to know what was going on. Rick calmly explained that he was working on a record and needed these people to sing on it. When told that it was late and he certainly couldn't be at it in the hotel hallway, he replied that he couldn't do it in his room. His roommate was sleeping—he had an early gig the next day and Rick didn't want to disturb him.

It is driving the long night highway with the huge responsibility of having some of the world's finest musicians on board.

It's how the team comes together year after year, finding any excuse to make the work good for one another. Like after a long hard, hot and busy summer, most of the Celtic Colours staff move out of their office in Sydney and set up on site at the festival. But some are always left behind to deal with business and the comings and goings of volunteers. In the early years it was Marg LeBlanc who looked after the office and ticketing. One year, Nigel was feeling bad about Marg missing out on all the action, the fun part of it anyway, at the Festival Club—so he came up with "International Marg Day." At the end of the festival, without telling her why, we brought Marg up to the Gaelic College for the last night of Festival Club.

"I had taken the festival's Celtic knot logo and superimposed a picture of Marg's face on it," says Nigel. "Then we printed it out as big as we could and put it up on the wall at the Festival Club." It was nothing more than an inside joke, the staff's heartfelt tribute to Marg who had worked so hard during those years.

In her own inimitable manner, Marg thanked everyone with "You people have too much time on your hands." Or words very much like that.

My Celtic Colours is night without end, mornings that go on into the day. The sounds still in your head. And the aching, laughing, teasing goodbyes—some for now, and some forever.

And we are left to mourn those we've lost, and remember the best of times, thankful for the terrific sounds still ringing in our ears.

And me?—I've got to get some sleep.

*10 Nights Without Sleep* continues. For a list of those who performed at Celtic Colours, large photographs and additional information go to:

http://capebretonbooks.ca/10nightswithoutsleep/celticcoloursbook/

# Sources

PAGE

11 Tom Knapp, "Max MacDonald & Joella Foulds: Team Cape Breton," www. rambles.net, 2004

13 Celtic Colours International Festival program 1997

13 Poem based on "My Cape Breton Home" in *Cape Breton's Lillian Crewe Walsh: A Treasury of Ballads and Poems*, Breton Books, 2006

14 Frank Macdonald, "Celtic Colours Kickoff: Natalie, The Chieftains and Most of Mabou," *The Inverness Oran*, 1997

15 Gerry Wright, "Good Times Away: Celtic Colours CB," *The Buzz*, 1997

15 Tera Camus, "Chieftains Bring 3,500 to Feet," *Halifax Herald*, 1997

17 Paul MacDonald, "From Galway to Cape Breton: The Music of Sharon Shannon," *What's Goin On*, 1997

17 Bertha Ann MacLean, "Fosgail An Fhéis!", *What's Goin On*, 1997

18 Frank Macdonald, "Celtic Colours Kickoff," *The Inverness Oran*, 1997

18 Tera Camus, "Chieftains Bring 3,500 to Feet," *Halifax Herald*, 1997

18 Sharon Montgomery, "Celtic Colours Attracts Crowd: Music Fans Enthusiastic About Opening of Island Music Festival," *Cape Breton Post*, 1997

19 Bertha Ann MacLean, "Fosgail An Fhéis!", *What's Goin On*, 1997

19 Sharon Montgomery, "Celtic Colours Attracts Crowd," *Cape Breton Post*, 1997

19 Tom Knapp, "Max MacDonald & Joella Foulds," www.rambles.net, 2004

20 "Festival Rooted in Cape Breton's Culture," Celtic Colours press release, 1997

20 Ronald Caplan, "Jerry Holland: Fathers and Son," *Talking Cape Breton Music*, Breton Books, 2006

21 Frank Ferrel, "Fiddler's Heaven," *New England Folk Almanac*, 1997

23 Celtic Colours International Festival program, 1997

24 Iain Kenneth MacLeod, *What's Goin On*, 1997

24 Glenn Graham, *The Cape Breton Fiddle: Making and Maintaining Tradition*, Cape Breton University Press, 2006

26 Barry W. Shears, *The Cape Breton Collection of Bagpipe Music*, Taigh a' Chiuil/The House of Music, 1995

27 Ronald Caplan, "A Visit with Piper Alex Currie," *Talking Cape Breton Music*, Breton Books, 2006

28 Michael Grey, liner notes, *Fosgail an Dorus*, Gigs & Reels Productions, 1992

28 Iain Kenneth MacLeod, *What's Goin On*, 1997

28 Ronald Caplan, "A Visit with Piper Alex Currie," *Talking Cape Breton Music*

29 Iain Kenneth MacLeod, *What's Goin On*, 1997

30 "Festival Rooted in Cape Breton's Culture," Celtic Colours press release, 1997

32 "Community Volunteers Gear Up for Celtic Colours," Celtic Colours press release, 1997

PAGE

33 Frank Macdonald, *The Inverness Oran*, 1997

36 Based on Parker Barss Donham, "Celtic Colours, Cape Breton, Nova Scotia," 1998

40 "Guitar Summit," Dougie Johnson, *What's Goin On*, 1997

40 Frank Macdonald, "Celtic Colours Winds Up: A Thrilling Beginning to an Annual Event," *The Inverness Oran*, 1997

52 Tom Knapp, "Songs & Anecdotes of Gaelic Scotland with Margaret Bennett," workshop at Nova Scotia Highland Village, Iona, www.rambles.net, 2005

55 Tom Knapp interview with Wendy MacIsaac, www.rambles.net, 2003

56 Kaitlin Hahn, www.rambles.net

56 Mike Morrison, "Invasion of the Sleepless Funnytalkers," *What's Goin On*, 1998

60 Kelley Edwards, "This Magic Moment," *What's Goin On*, 1998

67 Tom Knapp

67 Tony McManus's online diary, 2001

69 Sandy MacDonald, "Behind the Beat," *The Daily News*, June 22, 2000

87 "A Day in the Life of a Celtic Colours Driver" is courtesy of Gerardette and Blair Brown

99 Tom Knapp

104 Tom Knapp

105 Wanda Earhart in *What's Goin On*

127 Victor Maurice Faubert, http://vmfaubert.com/

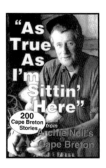